THE UNCHAINED
True Stories From Hillsboro, Oregon

Evergreen Christian Center

Published in Beaverton, Oregon, by Good Catch Publishing.
www.goodcatchpublishing.com
V1.1

Printed in the United States of America

Table of Contents

DEDICATION

Dedicated to God's life-changing love and the people of Evergreen, whose humble hearts reveal his glory through their life stories.

ACKNOWLEDGEMENTS

I would like to thank Pastor Marc Shaw for the prayer and faith he put into this book to make it a reality; Yuzuru Tanakura for the vision he had from the beginning and the hard work he put into making this book come to life; and the people of Evergreen Christian Center for their boldness and vulnerability in telling the stories that comprise this compilation of their real-life stories.

This book would not have been published without the amazing efforts of our project manager, Nanette Owen. Her untiring resolve pushed this project forward and turned it into a stunning victory. Thank you for your great fortitude and diligence. I would also like to thank our invaluable proofreader, Melody Davis, for all the focus and energy she has put into perfecting our words. Lastly, I want to extend our gratitude to Scott Boley, Evergreen's graphic artist, whose talent and vision is astounding.

Daren Lindley
President and CEO
Good Catch Publishing

The book you are about to read is a compilation of
authentic life stories.
All the facts are true, and all the events are real.
These storytellers have dealt with crisis, tragedy, abuse
and neglect and have shared their most private moments,
mess-ups and hang-ups in order for others to learn
and grow from them.
In order to protect the identities of those involved in their
pasts, the names of some storytellers have been
withheld or changed.

INTRODUCTION

We live in a fast-service society. We've been conditioned to expect immediate results, speedy service and a quick fix. Speedy and efficient service is not all bad, but when that translates to an expectancy of a "quick fix" in life struggles, it can be disappointing at best and potentially destructive. All of us want to take a quick way out: "Can't somebody just fix this?" We escape into unhealthy habits and addictions instead of facing our problems head on. No wonder we find ourselves mired in the muck of our difficulties with life — and its pain.

Depression, pain, humiliation, distress, grief and regret are increasingly common descriptions for our lot in life. Regardless of your age, culture, race or gender, everyone faces some of life's hurts, pains, knocks and bruises, hoping to get healing and relief — and move on. And although lasting life lessons may be learned, it so often seems like you are stuck in a hopeless process while you're going through it. So the questions remain: "Am I stuck? Is this all there is? Is life mainly about pain, and is the future hopeless for me?"

The following stories are about everyday people, like you, experiencing life's emotionally complicated and painful offerings, usually not of their own device or choices. Nevertheless, for them, they were the reality of life. Healing is a process. And though they have suffered, they have overcome these struggles and are no longer dominated by their haunting pasts. Our heart's cry is that you will find this book inspiring, encouraging and helpful in the midst of dealing with your life's challenges. And may you find an answer to your questions: "Am I stuck? Is this all? What can I do?"

HEALING SCARS
The Story of Amir
Written by Karen Koczwara

"What do you think would happen if I pulled this trigger?" My cousin twirled the little black handgun between his fingers inches away from my face.

I swallowed hard, slowly backing away from him. Was he joking? "I don't think I'd mess with that if I were you," I croaked. "Put it down, man."

He let out a low laugh and leaned back on his bed, tossing the gun up and down as though it were a football. "C'mon. You dare me to pull it?"

"Where did you even get that thing? This isn't funny, man. Put that down." I inched toward the bedroom door, my heart pounding. When my cousin said he had something to show me, this wasn't what I'd had in mind. I wanted to get out of there, and fast, but I didn't want him to do anything stupid. "Put it down, man," I repeated, panic rising in my voice.

He laughed again, a sort of sad, whimsical laugh, and then, in one quick motion, he spun the gun around, pointed it straight at his head and pulled the trigger. Blood spurted everywhere as his body went limp and fell with a thump to the ground.

I opened my mouth to scream, but nothing came out. I remained frozen, petrified, covered in sticky dark red blood. A dead body lay only inches from my feet, a body that had been very much alive only seconds ago. This must be some sort of nightmare! This didn't just happen! My entire body began to shake heavily, and I felt I might pass out at any moment. For a horrible brief second, I allowed my eyes to rest on his, wide open and lifeless, staring at me like a doll in a museum. How could he be dead?

The gun slipped from his limp hand and onto the carpet, where blood pooled around him and seeped toward me like a jagged river. What if that gun had been turned on me? Just like that, I could have died. Again, I tried to open my mouth to scream, but nothing came out ...

***

"Hey! What are you doing, boy?" My father grabbed my shirt collar and glared hard at me. "Did you take that lollipop from your brother just now?"

I trembled, my little 5-year-old knees going weak at the sight of my father so angry. My father was angry most of the time — one of the byproducts of his shame-based upbringing — but this time, he looked especially upset. I glanced around the little park frantically, searching for my mother to come alongside me and rescue me. "I'm sorry," I mumbled, bowing my head.

"Sorry? Sorry isn't good enough! Always doin' what you're not supposed to be doin', getting yourself into trouble. You look at your brother right now and say you're sorry!" my father growled, tugging on my collar and turning me around to face my brother.

"I, I'm sorry I took your lollipop," I said quietly, trying

not to cry. Crying was a sign of weakness to my father.

My brother shrugged and started sucking on his lollipop, clearly unfazed by the incident. My father, however, was not done with me. "I didn't hear you, boy!" he hollered again, yanking my collar so hard this time I feared he might choke me.

"I said sorry!" I repeated loudly. *Please leave me alone*, I prayed.

"You should be." My father released his grip on me, and I breathed a sigh of relief. "You stupid boy!" In one swift motion, he pushed me to the ground and kicked me in the chest. Hard.

I reeled from the pain as I tried to regain my breath, clutching my tiny legs to my chest and rocking back and forth. Tears poured down my cheeks as I screamed. I hated my father, hated him for being so cruel. Why was he always so cruel when I tried so hard to please him? "Owww!" I sobbed. "You hurt me!"

"Serves you right for being so bad!" my father snarled, glaring down at me with his dagger eyes. "Maybe next time you'll think twice before you do something stupid."

"What on earth is going on here?" Suddenly my mother was by my side, terror in her eyes. She held my hand and whirled to face my father angrily. "Did you just kick him?" she screamed. "How dare you? Look what you did!"

"You best be quiet, woman," my father retorted, pushing her aside. "Your son here can't seem to keep his hands to himself. Had to put him in his place!"

THE UNCHAINED

My brother stood quietly, his head bowed, hands shoved in his pockets. I watched him from the corner of my eye and knew he was just as terrified as I was. We had both seen our father angry, but never to this degree. Pain shot through my chest as I tried to pick myself off the muddy ground, not sure whether my soul or my body hurt more.

A couple of large men who had been kicking a ball around near the playground came running over. "We saw what you just did," the one man growled, inching toward my father like a lion ready to jump on his prey. "You'd better not move, because someone in that house across the street saw, too, and just called the cops."

"This is none of your business!" my father shouted, putting up his fist as though he was ready to fight. "Get out of here now! This ain't your boy here."

"Doesn't matter. You can't go kicking a child. He's just a child! How old are you, boy?" The one man looked down at me kindly. "Four?"

"Five," I whispered, brushing away my tears.

"Get up, boy. We're going home." My father yanked me off the ground and turned to my mother. "Now! In the car!"

Just then, I heard sirens and looked up to see two police cars screeching to the sidewalk. Were they really coming for my father? Would they take him away from us? A mixture of fear and excitement welled in my chest as I scooted toward my brother, who stood silently sucking his lollipop. He looked like he had just seen an unforgettable horror flick.

"Over here!" the one man hollered, motioning the policemen toward us as they ran.

"Put your hands in the air!" the cop called out. "Don't move, sir!"

My father had been an enraged man for as long as I could remember. I felt I could never please him, no matter what I did. I tried my best to get good grades in school, be kind to my siblings and work hard around the house, but it was never enough. Growing up in a Muslim household made it especially difficult. Muslim men believed women should be set in their place and remain silent and children should follow strict rules without uttering a complaint, under any circumstances. I lived in constant fear of my father, wondering what I would do next to cause his wrath to escape.

Shortly after my father was arrested, my parents divorced. My mother simply could not live under my father's impossible rules. They went to court, and my father obtained partial custody of my brother, sister and me. I was devastated. I would have been completely happy to live with my mother full-time and never see my father again. My mother, who had been raised a Christian, converted to Islam when she married my father. It was not an option for my mother to continue living a Christian lifestyle; she could have been killed for her beliefs.

I continued to bounce back and forth between my parents' households, but always dreaded my visits with my father. I often lay awake at night in bed, wondering when he was going to fling open my door and yell at me.

"Why did you get a B on that test, son? Didn't you study? You worthless, stupid boy!" my father growled one night, storming into my room with fire in his eyes.

I trembled beneath the covers, glad it was dark so he couldn't see my pale face and the tears that already started to spill down my cheeks. How I hated him! "I'll do better next time," I squeaked. "It was a hard test!"

"I'll do better next time," my father mocked, kicking my dresser so hard one of the drawers nearly fell out onto the ground. "Boy, you better shape up around here! Right now, you're good for nothing, you hear me?"

"Yes, sir," I replied, licking salty tears that trickled into my mouth. "I'm sorry." I felt like a robot, always saying I was sorry, I would do better next time and I would try harder. Deep down, though, I knew no matter how hard I tried, I'd somehow fail him. There was never a "good enough" with my father.

When I was 9 years old, my best friend called me one afternoon after school. "What do you really think is out there in life?" he asked me.

I thought it was a sort of odd question, very philosophical for such a young boy. "I dunno. I never thought much about it," I replied slowly. "Why do you ask?"

"Just thinking about things. I think I want to kill myself."

I laughed, sure he was joking. "What are you talking about? Why would you say that?"

"I just think I want to kill myself," he repeated. "I wonder how far the fall from the bridge will be." He sounded serious, but I was sure he was just joking. Why on earth would a 9 year old be thinking about death?

"Well, if you really want to die, just wait a few more years. Eventually, everyone dies," I replied lightheartedly. "I gotta go finish my homework before my dad yells at me. See you tomorrow at school, all right?" I hung up and shook my head, baffled by our short but bizarre conversation.

The next day at school, my best friend's seat was empty. I didn't think much of it. A nasty flu bug had been going around school, and I figured he had caught it. When he didn't show up the next day, though, I began to worry a bit.

That night, as my sister and I flipped through the news stations on the television, she paused at a police report about a young boy who had committed suicide when he jumped from a local bridge. My heart stopped in my chest as I glanced up at the picture flashed on the screen: It was a picture of my best friend. Dead at 9 years old.

"Isn't that boy in your class?" my sister asked, leaning forward.

As the newscaster rattled on about a storm that was coming in, I continued to stare straight ahead in shock. It couldn't be true! I had just spoken with him two days ago. I thought for sure he was joking. How could someone so young want to jump from a bridge?

When my father entered the room several minutes later, he found me still staring at the TV screen, wide-eyed and unable to move. "What are you doing, boy? Get up! You've got homework to finish" he growled in his usual disapproving tone.

I didn't blink. "What … does … it … mean … to … die?" I whispered.

"Huh? What are you talking about, boy?"

"His best friend just killed himself. It was just on the news," my sister replied for me, jumping to her feet and scampering out of the room.

"You okay, boy?" For a moment, my father seemed to let his guard down as he sat down next to me and slipped an awkward arm around my shoulder. "You knew that boy, huh?"

I nodded numbly. "He was my best friend. He's dead."

"Death is a final thing, son. That boy made a very foolish choice." My father went on to explain what it meant to die. I listened with one ear, still in shock from what I had just seen and heard. My best friend killed himself, after he called me with a cry for help! If only I had listened to him, perhaps he would still be alive. I was devastated.

***

When I got a bit older, I returned to Egypt to visit my relatives there. Both my parents were from Egypt and had moved to the northwestern United States after they married. Many of my grandparents and aunts and uncles still lived there, and I always enjoyed returning to the land where my family had so much heritage. While I did not particularly embrace Islam, I always obeyed its teachings — growing up in a Muslim household meant I really did not have much choice in the matter. Going against such a powerful religion could have resulted in serious consequences. I was too afraid of my father to find out what those might entail.

On this particular visit, one of my cousins convinced me to come upstairs with him to his bedroom, as he said he had something to show me. Expecting him to show me a new game or something, I was surprised when he closed the door firmly and pulled what looked to be a cigarette from his pocket. "Ever tried one of these?" he asked slyly, lighting the end of it.

An unusual smell filled the room as smoke began to coil toward me. "That's some powerful cigarette," I muttered, inching toward the door.

"It's not just any cigarette," he replied, laughing. "Marijuana, man. You never smoked dope before?"

I shook my head, feeling rather stupid for being so naive. "No."

"You gotta try this stuff. It goes straight to your head and gives you a great buzz." He shoved the cigarette at my face, and I winced.

I had seen plenty of people smoking, but this was all new to me. "Is that stuff legal?" I whispered. I could almost taste the smoke on my tongue.

"It is here, man. That's the beauty of it all. C'mon. Take a drag. You'll like it."

I shrugged and took it from him, holding it awkwardly

to my lips. "Like this?"

"Yeah. Now suck in, take a long drag and then slowly exhale. Take your time."

I did as he said, nearly gagging on the stuff as it burnt my lungs going down. A loud cough escaped my chest, and my eyes began to water. "I dunno, it's kinda strong," I muttered, shoving it back at him.

"You gotta give it another try," he coaxed. "You'll get used to it. Once you get hooked, you won't want to stop. I can get this stuff real cheap, so anytime you want it, you just say the word."

I felt as though I had been let into a secret world I hadn't known previously existed. My head began to throb, but I didn't want to look like a wimp in front of my cousin. I took the joint back and took another drag, then another. Before long, I became giggly and fell back onto the bed, rolling with laughter. "That stuff's pretty good, man," I said. "Not bad at all."

"Told you so." My cousin looked proud as he pulled out another joint and lit it.

I continued smoking pot even after I returned to the United States. I liked the quick buzz it gave me and how it allowed me to escape from my tormented world at home temporarily. I often found myself making funny or rude remarks, which later embarrassed me when I became sober again. I didn't feel like stopping, though. Besides, I reasoned, it wasn't really a drug. It was legal overseas, and it was really just a plant. There were much worse things in life.

HEALING SCARS

When I was 15, I met my first girlfriend. She was a sweet girl from a Christian family, and we grew close over the year we dated. I confided in her my dad was verbally abusive toward me, and she told me her parents were very hard on her, as well. She said her mother did not accept her for who she was. It was a common bond that drew us closer in our relationship.

"I feel like I can't do anything right in my mother's eyes," she told me often.

"I feel the same about my father," I replied sadly. "No matter what I do, I am not good enough for him."

One evening, I decided to surprise my girlfriend by taking her out to a romantic dinner. I took care to dress in my nicest clothes and bought a beautiful bouquet of flowers from a local vendor on my way to pick her up. With the stars winking at me in the sky as I headed off to her house, I had a feeling everything was going to turn out splendidly that evening.

"These are beautiful," she murmured when she opened her door, taking the flowers from me. "Let me put them in some water and we can go." She glanced back nervously and disappeared for a few moments.

I took her to one of my favorite pizza joints, where we scooted into a corner table and enjoyed the soft Italian music that played in the background. As I reached across the table to gently take her hand, she flinched and pulled away.

"Are you all right tonight?" I asked her. "You seem kind of jittery."

THE UNCHAINED

"I'm fine," she replied shortly, and put her nose back in the menu.

As the evening wore on, she grew more and more edgy. Our conversation was strained, and she seemed quite distracted throughout dinner, avoiding my eyes when she spoke. After dinner, I suggested a nice stroll along the river, and she complied.

I cracked a few jokes as we walked along, enjoying the nice cool breeze and the crisp evening air. "Are you having a good time?" I asked hopefully. I tried so hard to create a perfect evening, and yet she seemed like she was off in her own world.

"Fine," she murmured. Then, in an abrupt move, she pulled away from me and ran toward the edge of the bridge, climbing up onto the ledge. Her tiny frame swayed dangerously on top of the metal rungs as she looked down.

"What are you doing?" I screamed. "Get down from there! Are you crazy?"

And then, in what felt like slow motion, I watched her body fall forward from the bridge into the river dozens of feet below. My heart stopped as I raced toward the edge, unable to believe what just happened before my very eyes. "Noooo!" I cried out, falling weakly against the railing as I stared down below into the torrential waters. Her body was nowhere in sight. Just like that, she was gone. I fell to my knees and wept. "Noooo, noooo, noooo!" I moaned over and over. How could this have happened?

After that horrible moment, I began to grow numb to life. I experienced so much tragedy and heartache in my short life and wondered if I would be able to go on. I continued to smoke pot, enjoying the temporary high it gave me, taking me out of my sad reality for just a few moments. I went back and forth from my mother and father's house, always dreading the visits with my father because they meant more ridicule and torment.

One evening, I closed the door to my bedroom and crawled up onto my bed with a knife in my pocket. My hand trembled as I pulled it out and inspected the sharp blade, wondering how it would feel if I dug it into my skin. At that moment, my life flashed before my eyes: my father's constant verbal abuse, the people who had taken their lives before my very eyes, the drugs that consumed me as I sought comfort from the pain. Life didn't seem much worth living at that moment, and before I could change my mind, I made a single slice on my left arm. A drop of blood spurted out, and then another. I watched it trickle down my arm, and a single tear escaped down my cheek.

"What's the point?" I muttered, to no one in particular. I stared at my arm for several moments, then made another small slice. The searing pain was not nearly as awful as the pain I felt in my own heart. With a sudden urge, I began to slowly carve my name in my arm, as though it were an art project. Thick red blood continued to trickle down my arm and pool onto my hands, and I winced each time the blade hit my skin.

When I finished my name, I slowly raised the knife to my throat until it was nearly touching my skin. My heart thudded as I considered what I was about to do. I didn't want to do it, but I didn't see how life could possibly be worth living. "Help me," I murmured, tears spilling down my cheeks. My hand trembled as I held the knife, which suddenly felt like heavy lead in my hands.

Slowly, I put down the knife, laying the bloody blade on the bed beside me. I knew then and there I didn't want to die, that despite my pain, I could not take my own life and have someone find me and experience what I had with those who took their own lives in front of me. A sense of relief washed over me as I squeezed my arm, which was now throbbing in pain.

Death had dangled in front of me so many times, and the thought that I could have ended my life moments from now suddenly terrified me. I eased back on the bed and pulled the covers up, thankful I had not made that choice.

It wasn't long after that I met a lovely girl who captured my heart. She told me she was a Christian and invited me to church with her one Sunday.

"I don't know. My family is Muslim and feels very strongly about exploring other religions. If my father found out I was attending a Christian church, he might kill me," I told her, wondering if she knew how literally I meant that.

"Please. I really want you to join me," she pleaded. "Just this once?"

"Okay," I agreed reluctantly. "But I'm really not sure this is a good idea."

Still, I was curious about her religion. I knew a little

about Christianity from my previous girlfriend, but I never explored it much because my family was so strict in its beliefs. It would be interesting to attend her church and see if this God who she spoke about was anything like the god of the Koran with which I was familiar.

"Welcome! We're so glad you're here!"

"We're so blessed to have you with us today!"

From the moment I first walked through the doors at Evergreen Christian Center, I was taken aback by the friendliness of the church members who greeted me. I had been afraid I would stick out like a sore thumb, but everyone welcomed me into the congregation as though I was family. I found this very intriguing and appealing.

I sat quietly in the pew with my girlfriend as the pastor spoke about God's great purpose for our lives and how we could find hope in him. For the first time in my life, it began to make a bit of sense. The pastor himself seemed especially happy and upbeat, as though he lived every moment to the fullest. I found myself wondering what he had that I was missing.

"Everyone is so happy here," I whispered to my girlfriend as the service came to a close.

"They are happy because they have the Lord in their lives," she replied, smiling. "They have the hope in knowing God will never leave or forsake them and they will go to live in heaven with him one day."

I soaked her words in, mulling them carefully as we drove home. I wanted to know more about this God, who seemed like someone these people knew personally, rather than a God who dished out rules and regulations from his great throne in the sky.

"Do you believe in miracles?" my girlfriend asked as we pulled up to her house.

I blinked, surprised by her question. "I don't know. I never thought much about it. Why do you ask?"

"Well, in the Bible, Jesus performed many miracles, like bringing people back from the dead. He was no ordinary man, but the son of God, sent from heaven to lead others on earth to God. To this day, there has been no one else on earth who has been able to do what he did. This is something that sets apart Christianity from other religions and helps us to know it is the truth."

"Hmmm." I was fascinated by this and wondered if my girlfriend was the one who knew the real truth.

The following Sunday, I returned to church with her, surprised at how eager I was to attend. Once again, everyone who greeted me was especially kind and friendly and seemed to be full of a joy I had never experienced in my life. When the service came to a close, my girlfriend leaned over and asked me if I would like to go into the prayer room with her.

"I guess so," I mumbled, not knowing quite what to expect.

Several elderly people huddled around the tiny room, praying and comforting one another when we stepped in. They greeted me and asked if they could pray for me. I nodded, still a bit unsure as to what I had come in here for.

"Dear Lord, we pray your blessing on this young man and ask that you heal any disabilities he might have," one man prayed, putting a hand on my shoulder.

I felt an almost immediate peace surrounding me as they closed with an "amen." Turning to my girlfriend, I grinned. "That felt good," I told her. Suddenly, there was a tingling in my ear, and I nearly jumped back.

"Are you all right?" she asked.

"Yeah, I just, uh … I just felt this weird sensation in my ear. Like a tingling or something." I had always been hard of hearing and had to wear a hearing aid the last several years. "I feel like I can hear clearly now," I added, baffled at what had just taken place the moment the prayer ended.

"Hey, can you come here for a minute?" My girlfriend motioned one of the men over to my side. "Can you say something to my boyfriend? Anything." Turning to me, she added, "Take out your hearing aids."

"God bless you, young man," he said, smiling.

"Oh my gosh! I can hear him clear as a bell!" I hollered in a voice much too loud for a prayer room. "I can hear! This is a miracle!" Turning to my girlfriend, I pulled her into a hug and began to dance around the room. "I can hear! I do believe in miracles! I do!"

It wasn't long after this that I decided I wanted to become a Christian and know this God who had become very real to me over the past few weeks. Following the sermon on a beautiful Sunday morning, at the pastor's invitation, I accepted Christ, asking him into my heart to be my

THE UNCHAINED

Savior. I felt more free and alive than I had in years. I found what had been missing in my life, and that was Christ, the great healer! I felt a peace seep into my heart and thanked God for his love for me, a sinner.

"I want to get baptized," I told my girlfriend after church one Sunday. I was excited about my newfound faith and wanted to proclaim it to the world.

"That would be awesome!" my girlfriend agreed.

I was baptized shortly thereafter, and my only regret was my father could not share in my beautiful moment.

I told my mother about my decision to convert to Christianity, and she was thrilled for me. "I am so happy for you, my son, but you must be very careful. As you know, your father would be furious if he found out you had converted from Islam. This is just not acceptable in our society. This must stay between me and you, or he could kill you."

I saw the graveness in my mother's eyes and knew she was terribly concerned for me. This did not stop me from wanting to sing from the rooftops about my newfound faith, though. I continued attending church regularly with my girlfriend and tried to learn as much as I could about the Bible and this loving God who was so different than the God I had grown up hearing about. Meanwhile, I also mustered the courage to move out of my father's house for good. I felt immensely free knowing I would not be under his constant ridicule and rules day in and day out.

One Sunday, my girlfriend, who suffered from scoliosis, leaned over to me and suggested we go to the prayer room to ask for prayer for her terrible back pain. "God healed you of your hearing problem. Maybe he will heal me, too," she said excitedly.

The men eagerly prayed for her in the prayer room after service, and as we headed home that afternoon, she told me for the first time in years she didn't have any back pain. "God doesn't always choose to heal, but I am so amazed when he does," she told me as we rejoiced over our answered prayer. "What an awesome God!"

I continued to revel in the freedom I found in Christ. After years of feeling I was never good enough for my father, I found a heavenly father who, despite my faults, loved me just as I was and was still there to love me at the end of each day and forgive me of my daily sins.

***

I continued to face many obstacles after I accepted Christ. Because of my race, many people I encountered assumed I was Muslim. Often times when I rode the bus to work, people would stop and ask me about the Koran, or make a comment about Islam. I excitedly shared with them I had become a Christian, and while many praised me for my brave decision, others seemed confused and shocked I would make such a bold move against Muslim society. Many of my Arab friends chose to no longer speak to me. While many of their comments and assumptions hurt me, I remained confident I had learned the truth and prayed they might one day find it, too.

THE UNCHAINED

Several months ago, I was faced with another terrible episode when I was accused of identity theft. A frequent eBay seller, I listed a computer for sale on eBay, and there was some confusion with the credit card information the site requested from the seller. I was shocked when a uniformed policeman showed up at my door one afternoon, informing me I was under arrest for two counts of felony charges: one for forgery and one for identity theft!

"Are you sure you have the right guy?" I asked, confused. "Perhaps there was some mistake made. I would never intentionally do something like that."

"Come with me, and I'll read you your rights," he replied coldly.

My heart raced wildly as the police car whizzed toward the station. I wracked my brain, trying to think what on earth I could have possibly done to merit this. The eBay transaction confusion came to mind, but I was sure there was no way it could have been mistaken as forgery and identity theft. I wasn't a criminal. I was simply a teenage boy trying to make a few bucks on an auction site!

The moment the cop escorted me into the station, I watched an aggravated man get tasered before my very eyes. That was terrifying, and I decided right then and there to cooperate and keep my mouth shut for the moment. I would have a chance to defend my innocence later, but for now, I had to work on getting out of here without incident.

The 24 hours inside those barren prison walls seemed like the longest hours of my entire life. I sat in a hard wooden chair in the corner of the room, tucking my legs beneath me and praying. I knew that surely there had to be some mistake and soon the truth would be known. I prayed God would help me stay strong, and amazingly, a sense of peace washed over me as I sat there, knowing he would act as my defender.

After what felt like an eternity, I was brought before the officials to plead my case. "I assure you I am innocent," I said adamantly. "I simply had a problem with my computer, and there was some confusion with the credit card transaction."

A uniformed man before me cleared his throat and nodded. "Gentlemen, at this point, we don't have enough evidence to charge this man with these felony counts. He may be released."

I breathed a sigh of relief as I stepped outside, appreciating the warm sunshine that fell onto my shoulders. "Thank you, Lord," I prayed.

A couple months later, I obtained a wonderful job as a 911 operator. I enjoyed taking calls from people each day, knowing I was helping them and making a difference in their lives. I was also thankful the felony charges had been cleared on my record; otherwise, I was certain I would not have obtained such a good-paying job.

At last, I mustered the courage to tell my father I had accepted Christ into my heart. I found myself knocking on his front door one afternoon, my entire body trembling as I heard his footsteps coming toward me. I knew if I did not confide in him, he would find out sooner or later and be even more livid than he might be if I told him myself. "Help me, God, to be strong," I prayed silently as the doorknob turned.

"You have done what?" My father looked enraged as I related to him I had become a Christian. "Son, do you know what this means? You have turned against our religion! The religion that my father embraced, and his father, and his father! How can you do this to our family?"

"I am nearly a grown man," I asserted bravely, sitting straight in my chair. "And I have made my choice. I am sorry, Father, if I have disappointed you. I pray someday you may know the truth as I know it." I knew my words angered him, but I felt hopeful nonetheless as I stepped outside his house that afternoon, a huge wave of relief washing over me as I started the car.

As I drove home that afternoon, I thought about my life and how much pain I suffered over the years. I had been living in constant fear of my father, hoping that one day, I could finally please him and do something right in his eyes. Meanwhile, my heavenly father had been waiting for me all along, never once telling me I wasn't good enough. It was amazingly freeing to know a God who would never let me down, who would stand by my side for the rest of my life.

I thought about the day I had been healed from my hearing problem inside that little prayer room. To some, it was probably a small miracle, but to me, it was life changing. I finally met the God of miracles, and the truth had set me free. Though I knew my struggles were far from over, I felt more hope than I ever had before.

I glanced down at the scar on my left arm, the scrawled letters that now serve as a reminder of the time I had nearly given up and taken my own life. Though the scar remained, the wounds are healed. Inside and out, God healed my wounds and made me new. And *that* is worth living for!

PRODIGAL
The Story of Julie Najdek
Written by Angela Prusia

"There was a man who had two sons. The younger one said to his father, 'Father, give me my share of the estate.' So he divided his property between them … the younger son got together all he had, set off for a distant country and there squandered his wealth in wild living."

Cocaine crystals glittered on the mirror like my diamond wedding ring. My gaze trailed down the thin white line and stopped on Jolene. We worked together at my new job.

"Try it, Julie." The words dripped off her tongue like venom. Faded red lipstick outlined cracked lips.

"Is that cocaine?" The alcohol was making me giddy, so a giggle came out as a snort.

"Just do it," Jolene smiled. Her charisma drew me to her. "You won't get drunk so fast."

I'd heard that cocaine mixed with alcohol raised a person's tolerance. The girls teased me for getting wasted after a couple beers. They were hardcore drinkers, so they didn't get drunk as easily. I'd only recently started to drink and wanted to please my new friends.

"Like this?" I ignored my screaming conscience and held the straw to the powder. My mother was probably on her knees right now for me, but I didn't care. All I felt was the loneliness. My husband of two years was out fishing with his buddies for the weekend, again, and I just wanted to fit in with my coworkers.

Jolene nodded. "Just inhale."

Why not? Cocaine probably wasn't much different from nicotine. I'd started smoking with the girls, too. I snorted the white crystals, imagining the euphoria I'd feel. I threw up instead.

"Don't worry," Jolene rubbed my shoulders. "You'll be a pro in no time." She nodded toward the girls. "Just like us."

The smell of my puke threatened to undo my stomach once again. I managed a weak smile, remembering other faces — faces that belonged to Cindy and Jennifer, my best friends since junior high. Our love for music united us. We wrote songs together and sang our hearts out as we toured with our Christian band. Cindy sang first soprano, I sang second and Jennifer sang alto. We were friends forever.

"Come on, I'll take you home," the voice interrupted my reverie. Jolene stuck out her hand, which was good since my legs wobbled underneath me. The next thing I remember is waking up in my empty bed, knowing I needed to shower to erase the evidence before my husband returned.

"Hey, honey." Ron pecked me on the cheek. He proudly displayed his catch. I wrinkled my nose at the smell. "Me and the boys had us some luck." He pushed open the back door. "How was your weekend?"

"Fine." My answer was lost as the door slammed shut. My worry disappeared. Ron hadn't suspected a thing. He was too busy gutting dead fish to have a real conversation, but for the first time in our marriage, I didn't feel the familiar ache.

***

"What do you think you're doing?" my husband exploded. The hardness on his face didn't mask the hurt in his eyes.

"It's not a big deal." I tried to shrug off the accusation.

"Not a big deal?" he screamed. "My little sister tells me you're doing drugs, and you don't see the problem?"

Denise had begged me to take her partying when I told her about my new friends. I was full of stories as she worked on my nails. Ron was mad enough; he didn't need to know any more details — like the fact that Denise had experimented with cocaine at my nudging.

"It's like I don't even know you anymore," Ron spit. A droplet landed on my cheek.

I started to argue with my husband, but he was right. I'd let my love grow cold. A chunk of ice covered my heart.

"You're not the woman I married." Ron spoke so softly, I almost didn't hear the words.

The truth stared me in the face, but the ice had touched more than my heart. My spirit had frozen, too. I wasn't the same naïve girl who'd always followed the rules, who'd given her heart to Jesus as a young child. The taboo enticed me, pulling me farther from my roots. I rather liked the new me.

"You need to choose," Ron demanded. "Me or them."

I closed the door behind me and spent the night at a hotel.

I didn't want to see Ron the next morning, but I needed to get my things. He met me at the door with red eyes.

"We need to talk," he gulped.

"Didn't we do that last night?" My lack of feeling surprised me.

"I'm sorry, Julie. I said some things I regret." Ron pleaded with me to stay, but I knew we were finished. I threw my clothes into my car.

"Please, Julie. I still love you."

I revved the engine. No sense prolonging the inevitable.

"We'll go to counseling," Ron called out as I took off.

I later agreed, but even counseling didn't help. Ron wouldn't change anymore than I would. When he told the counselor I had all the problems, our marriage was over. I'd learned to stuff a lot of things in my life after my father abandoned me; my feelings for Ron would be no different.

I moved in with a friend of a friend, a drug dealer. The chains were gone. I was free to party to my heart's content. And I did. Hard. For 15 years.

PRODIGAL

***

"This isn't like you, Julie. You went to youth group and worked at church camp."

I rolled my eyes. I was sick of my Christian friends trying to counsel me.

"How can you just walk away from your faith?" Jennifer asked. She pushed a strand of long dark hair from her eyes.

"Because I just don't know anymore, okay?"

Cindy looked like she could cry. "You don't believe in Jesus?"

I shrugged. "I have my doubts." The irony wasn't lost on me. I'd been the one to invite Cindy to church when we met in junior high.

"I don't understand." Jennifer was rock solid in her faith, just like I'd once been.

"Don't you remember when we read the book of Revelation in one night?" Jennifer's big brown eyes met mine.

I'd almost forgotten. We'd read the book when I'd spent the night at her house. My spirit stirred as the Bible came alive.

"I can't watch you do this," Jennifer sniffled. "You're my friend, and I can't bear to see you get hurt."

Whatever. She obviously didn't know the pleasure drugs brought.

"We'll pray for you," Cindy whispered into my hair as she hugged me.

They could join my mother, my grandmother, my sister and her kids. I was through listening.

I bought a six-pack and toasted my absent father. The psychiatrists would say my issues revolved around my feelings of abandonment. He and my mother divorced when I was 12. Since they fought behind closed doors, the news came as a shock. Later, I found out about the other woman my father chose over us.

Pain ripped through me as I left Hawaii to start another life in Oregon with my mother's family. My grandfather tried to step in where my dad stepped out, but my trust lay shattered in a million pieces.

I had to be the strong one when my mother was a puddle on the floor or my sister lashed out in anger. The weight of this responsibility forced me to grow up. I went through numerous boyfriends before I settled on my high school sweetheart. I was 18 when Ron and I married.

If only we hadn't strayed away from the church …

If only we hadn't started to drink …

If only I'd told Ron how I felt abandoned when he left me for those long fishing weekends …

A series of small decisions stripped away the foundation my mother set, and I chose the same destructive path my father followed.

***

"After he had spent everything, there was a severe famine in that whole country, and he began to be in need. So he went and hired himself out to a citizen of that country, who sent him to his fields to feed pigs. He longed to fill his stomach with the pods that the pigs were eating, but no one gave him anything."

"You're shameless," my roommate yelled over the noise in the bar. She was upset I was going to leave with three guys I'd just met, but I was high, it was late, and I wanted to get laid.

"I thought you said he was disgusting," she pleaded.

I laughed. "Everybody gets better looking the longer the night goes on."

Dan winked at me. "You ready, little lady?"

I stumbled off the bar stool and followed Dan and his friends out to the empty parking lot. The four of us piled into Dan's truck and peeled out of there. Not only was I alone with three guys I didn't even know, I'd left my purse in my roommate's car, so I had nothing except the ID in my pocket. I was too wasted to think of my stupidity.

We drove out to the country before Dan dropped off his friends, then took me to his trailer.

"You ready for a good time, baby?" Dan asked.

I giggled, and he threw me on the bed. "Shh!" Dan covered my mouth. "We'll wake up my mother."

"You live with your mother?" Disgust rose to the surface, then sunk with the rest of my rational thoughts. I had no more control of myself than a rat in a science experiment.

He kissed me hard, his saliva trailing down my face.

I was too wasted to protest. He was too plastered for

sex.

The next morning, I tripped over Dan's clothes on my way to the bathroom. I gagged at the stench of urine and avoided touching anything because of the filth. The sight of caked makeup brought a fresh wave of revulsion. I looked at my reflection, not sure who stared back. My hair stood out in multiple directions and black mascara ringed bloodshot eyes.

My teeth were furry, so I dabbed some toothpaste on my finger. I did the best I could with my hair and hurried to relieve myself. I had to get out of this hellhole.

"You hungry?" Dan was dressed and at the door — much to my relief.

I wanted to lie, but I could've eaten dog food, I was so famished. He drove to a nearby restaurant where I gobbled everything in sight, not bothering with manners. I really didn't care what Dan thought.

Dan took me home, and we had sex. I figured it was the least I could do after he paid for breakfast. A whore would've had more respect. I couldn't even remember what real love felt like, the kind of love I'd once shared with my husband. I'd forgotten the faces of half the guys I'd slept with, much less their names. Sex wasn't love; each act only ripped out my heart, leaving a brittle shell of low self-esteem.

✳✳✳

"When he came to his senses, he said, 'How many of

my father's hired men have food to spare, and here I am starving to death!'"

"I love you, Julie," Peter whispered in my ear one night at a party. He worked the lights for a local rock band.

Love was such a strong word, and my divorce was still too fresh.

"I like you, too," I told Peter. "But I'm not looking for a commitment right now."

Peter seemed to understand. His sister, one of my friends, had introduced us. I became one of the band's groupies to be with him, so Peter and I hooked up at a lot of the parties. When he showed up on my doorstep with flowers and balloons on my birthday, I was touched in a way I hadn't been in a long time. I moved in with Peter, and we lived together for three years.

While I abused drugs and alcohol, Peter had an addiction that scared me. Deep down, I knew I was headed down the same path. My habits were stupidly expensive and beginning to waste more than just weekends. If I didn't get thrown in jail, I'd lose my job.

"Where were you?" I screamed at Peter when he returned from a three-day binge.

Peter shrugged. "I don't know."

Anger surged within me. I smashed all our cocaine mirrors and threw the cocaine grinders and brass tooters into our small Weber grill. I doused it with lighter fluid and lit the fire, even though I knew they wouldn't burn. I was done with drugs, and I wanted to make a point.

THE UNCHAINED

"What'd you do that for?" Peter complained.

I was scared, but I didn't want to admit to Peter that I really loved him. "It's either me or the drugs." The scene was vaguely familiar.

Peter's jaw tightened.

"If you don't get help, I'm telling your family."

I'd struck a chord. "Fine. I'll get help."

Peter wouldn't check into rehab because he didn't want his family to know about his problems. "I'm gonna quit cold turkey," Peter told his counselor and then later me. "To prove to Julie how much I love her."

And he did. Six months later, we got married.

***

"While he was still a long way off, his father saw him and was filled with compassion for him; he ran to his son, threw his arms around him and kissed him."

"Julie!" the familiar voice screamed across the airport terminal.

I turned in surprise. Shame washed over me at the sight of the friend I'd rejected so many years ago.

"I've missed you so much." Cindy ran toward me with her arms outstretched. "It's so good to see you, Julie."

Emotion lodged in my throat. Though I'd lived with her for almost two months in high school when my mom got remarried, Cindy wasn't blood. Family had to stick by you. Friends didn't. And yet Cindy reached out to me even when I pushed her away. She wrote me letters — I didn't reply. She invited me to her wedding — I didn't go. And she sent me Christmas cards — I never responded.

I melted into Cindy's embrace. She was the best hugger on the planet. My spirit gasped for air. Here was unconditional love, the love I'd craved for so long.

"I want you to meet my kids," Cindy smiled, her auburn curls bobbing. Three bodies clustered around us.

The stain of my choices made me feel like dirt. Their innocence contrasted with my scum, yet Cindy wanted me to meet her children — Brandon, Sarah and Jordan. Something shifted inside me.

"Give me your number," Cindy said before she had to leave. "Now that I've found you, I'm not letting you go."

***

Over the next three years, God drew me back with only a tenderness the author of love could know. He freed me of my addictions to cocaine, alcohol and nicotine and nudged me back to his word. I started reading my Bible when a coworker gave me a copy of the monthly devotional, *The Upper Room*. Not only did the story of the prodigal son speak to me, Proverbs 3:5-6 became real. "Trust in the Lord with all your heart and lean not on your own understanding; in all your ways acknowledge him, and he will make your paths straight." I'd made a mess of my life. It was time to put my trust in Jesus.

I feared what church would do to my marriage. I'd

seen my mother attend church without my father and watched their marriage crumble. God connected me to fellow believers by reestablishing my friendships with Cindy and Jennifer. The three of us would often meet together for lunch at Applebee's or for an Orange Julius at the Lancaster Mall in Salem. We'd laugh and talk and cry and pray together as I gained my footing once again.

When I read a book called *God Works the Night Shift*, I found out the author pastored a church in Beaverton, so I began to attend. I absorbed the teachings but didn't put down roots. When I went to a funeral at Evergreen Christian Center and saw the people rejoice, I tucked away the thought that I could go to this church someday — though the drive to Hillsboro was more than I liked.

Shortly after the pastor's death from leukemia, God moved Peter and me to rural Hillsboro. My husband always wanted to live in the country, and a wonderful piece of property became available. I said goodbye to Beaverton on Easter Sunday in 2004. The following Wednesday, I walked into Evergreen Christian Center, heard the full band music and said, "Oh, yeah. I'm home." That Sunday, I signed up for a Tuesday night Bible study. I'd been gone too long; it was time to put down roots. The prodigal daughter was home.

***

"The son said to him, 'Father, I have sinned against heaven and against you. I am no longer worthy to be called your son.' But the father said to his servants, 'Quick! Bring the best robe … put a ring on his finger … bring the fattened calf … let's have a feast and celebrate … for this son of mine was dead and is alive again; he was lost and is found.'"

"Julie, you need to get here," Cindy rushed over the phone. "The baby's coming!"

I flew down the highway toward Eugene, praying I didn't get a ticket. I ran through the parking lot at the hospital.

"Where's the delivery room?" I asked the volunteer at the information desk.

She pointed the way, and I raced to the room, throwing on a hospital gown.

Cindy beamed from the hospital bed. She handed me a little bundle in a blue blanket. "Meet Jonathan."

"Hey, Johnnie-cakes," I cooed, looking into his precious face.

"Jennifer already agreed."

I cocked my head. "Agreed to what?"

"To be Jonathan's godmother." Cindy smiled. "Say you will be, too."

"Me?" I choked down the tears and nodded.

A tiny fist wrapped around my fingers.

"Auntie Julie's gonna be praying for you, Jonathan. Just ask your sister and brothers. Their auntie's already been on her knees for them."

THE UNCHAINED

"Smile." Cindy's husband snapped a picture. I couldn't have grinned any wider.

***

"Julie, have you ever thought about teaching Sunday school?" Jeri asked me. The two of us had gotten close through our Bible study group.

I hesitated.

"We have an opening in the fifth and sixth grade room."

"I don't know," I sighed. How could God use someone like me? I felt so unworthy.

"You'd be so awesome," Jeri encouraged me. "Your love for Jesus pours from you."

I thought of my favorite verse in Luke. "Her many sins have been forgiven — for she loved much. But he who has been forgiven little, loves little." How could I not love much? My filth was washed clean by the blood of my Redeemer. I was never leaving home again.

"I'm not who you think I am," I told Jeri.

She raised her eyebrows.

I told her my story, sure that my past disqualified me.

"You're a child of the King." Jeri wrapped her arms around me. "If God has forgiven you, why shouldn't we?"

Tears filled my eyes. Now, three years later, I see God using me in the lives of children. When they come to me with life's tough questions and the choices they are facing, I've been able to share my story. Because my husband's

battle with testicular cancer made having children difficult, I treasure my spiritual children.

God is using me in other ways, as well. Both my father
and former pastor died of leukemia, so I'm working with
cancer fundraising efforts. I have a new goal: to walk the
Portland Marathon, so God is using me to pray for the
people of Portland as I walk through the city streets.

I also pray for my husband. God's word says that an
unbelieving husband may be won over by the behavior of
his wife. Though it's sometimes challenging to bite my
tongue, my husband knows something has changed in my
life. He comments on my joy and the peace that permeates
our home. He also appreciates that I don't cram God
down his throat. I can't wait to see what God's got in store
for Peter.

Sometimes dark forces remind me of my past, but God
keeps pursuing me, wooing me. Nothing I've done can
separate me from the love of Christ. I've always been his
child, but when I rejected him, he let me go, even though
he watched from the sidelines. His protection alone saved
me from certain death. Then, when I was ready to come
home, Jesus stretched out his arms and ran to me.

A LITTLE HELP FROM ABOVE
The Story of Lori Neitz
Written by Karen Koczwara

I'm going to die! I screamed the words in my mind, but my mouth remained frozen as I began tumbling downward through the air, legs flailing. *No, God. Please!* My heart thudded in my chest as I closed my eyes for just a moment, unable to watch the ground below me while the patchwork quilt of hilly terrain grew closer and closer. Surely it was not my time to go. I was too young!

My mind raced to my girls, my two beautiful daughters who begged me not to embark on this trip this morning. Why, oh, why, hadn't I listened to them? They had been so sure something would go wrong. *Please, God, let me live so I can raise my girls. There's no one else but me!* Tears stung my eyes as I gasped for air, my chest burning from the high altitude.

Blinking open my eyes, I looked down with horror while the ground beneath me grew closer, my inevitable fate just moments away. *Please, God, let me live!* Once again, no words came to my lips, but the words rang loud and clear in my mind. Just one more chance to live! I had so much to do still, so many dreams to fulfill.

My heart thudded in synch with the flapping chutes behind me, and I felt myself spinning more and more out of control. The ground below taunted me, as though it was waiting for my arrival, ready to envelop me and bring me to my death. Once more, I pleaded in my mind. *God,*

THE UNCHAINED

please, let me live. Oh, please, please let me live.

∗∗∗

"Come on, everyone! The Rose Parade is about to start any minute!" my mother hollered from the living room, where she sat huddled next to our little television.

"Breakfast is almost ready. Just a minute!" my dad hollered back.

I hopped up, eager to help my father. Just 3 years old, I loved watching my parents as they worked in the kitchen. If I was lucky, they might let me stir the batter, butter the bread or crack an egg. I skipped into the little kitchen and drug a chair over to the stove, where my father stood over a pan of bacon, whistling as he scooted the sizzling meat back and forth with a spatula.

"Lori! Hi, sweetheart!" My father spun around, his warm eyes meeting mine as I nestled up next to him. My father was a firefighter, a strong man who always made me feel safe and protected. I loved being near my father. "Did you come in to help Daddy? I've got us some bacon cooking on the stove. Your favorite!"

I smiled up at my father and nodded. "Yummy!"

My mother bustled into the kitchen, followed by several of my relatives. "Are we out of orange juice?" she asked, flinging open the refrigerator. "Oh, never mind, I see some in the back here. Need a hand, dear? We're all getting hungry."

"Should be just another minute," my father replied,

winking at me. "I've got a little helper here."

I loved New Year's Day. Though I was too young to understand what significance it bore, I knew it was a cozy day filled with delicious food, beautiful floats on TV and family gathered around the living room to chat and play. I could hardly wait to cuddle up next to my mother on the living room floor and bite into a large juicy slice of bacon.

"Watch out!" Suddenly, as if in slow motion, the sizzling hot pan of bacon grease flew into the air and landed squarely on my head. I let out a piercing scream as I felt my skin on fire. Everything around me went black; I felt like my entire head had been burned with boiling hot water. "Ahh!" I let out another piercing scream, which was shortly followed by my father's and then my mother's.

"Oh, baby, baby!" I felt my mother's cool hands on me as she rushed me across the room, while my father continued to scream. "Lori! Oh, Lori!"

Suddenly, it felt as if my entire body was going numb; I began to shake uncontrollably and whimper. "Mama, Mama, Mama!" I croaked, groping for her hand. Blackness enveloped me while the kitchen transformed itself into a horror scene.

"She's burned badly!"

"We've got to get her to the hospital. There's no time to waste!"

"Hurry! Someone help me!"

I felt a splash of cool water on my face, but its momentary refreshment was replaced by a painful sting. At just 3 years old, I didn't understand much, but I did know two things: something terrible just happened, and I was burned badly.

"It's going to be okay, baby, just hang in there," my mother whispered frantically, patting me down with another cool towel. "Mama's going to get you help."

"I can't take her. I can't see this. This is all my fault!" I heard my father's voice, just above a wail, from across the room. My daddy's fault? This was all my daddy's fault? Surely not my big, strong firefighter daddy.

"Someone find my car keys. We can't waste a minute," my mother hollered, scooping me up in her arms. I threw my tiny arms around her neck and wished more than anything the pain would stop. I knew this was something even the biggest Band-Aid couldn't heal.

"I'm sorry, I can't go. I'm so sorry," I heard my father utter as we fled the kitchen. My little body bobbed up and down under my mother's awkward grip as we headed for the car. I tried to open my eyes, but it felt as if my eyelids were glued shut. What was happening to me?

"Mama, I'm scared," I whimpered as my mother lifted me into the car and set me down on the cold vinyl seat. "I can't see!"

"Oh, baby, you're going to be okay. I promise." My mother seemed to say the words as if to assure herself. I heard the engine rumble, and then moments later, the little car screeched out of the driveway. "Mama's taking you to the hospital. The doctors are going to make you all better. I promise."

The next few hours were a blur of strange sounds,

noises and feelings. Drifting in and out of sleep, I heard bits and pieces of the doctors' conversations.

"Ma'am, I am sorry to inform you that your daughter is most likely going to be blind and disfigured for the rest of her life," the doctor murmured to my mother as they stood hovered over my bedside.

"Blind and disfigured?" Agony crept into my mother's voice as she clamped her hand over mine. "Oh, dear God."

"I'm so sorry. Those are some terrible burns. Your daughter is lucky it was not any worse. She may not have survived."

Laying there, my tiny frame enveloped by cloths, wires and bandages, I knew my life would never again be the same.

As the weeks and months went by, I amazed even the most skeptical doctors by how well my body healed and responded to the burn treatments. I regained my eyesight, much to the delight of my emotionally exhausted parents.

"I was on watch," my father told my mother on more than one occasion, speaking in firefighter lingo. "I should not have let that happen to my own daughter." My father continued to blame himself for the horrible accident, since he had been the one to let the bacon grease fly from the pan and hit me in the face. I did not love my father any less because of what happened, though. In my eyes, he was still the same strong, loving man he had always been.

When I grew a bit older and entered school, I came to realize I did not look quite the same as the other children. Though the scars on my face healed remarkably well, I still had a large patch of hair missing on one side of my head where every single hair had been burned in the accident. I tried my best to comb my hair from the other side over each morning in hopes that it would cover the bald spot. It wasn't long, however, before the children discovered my missing hair and began to taunt me on the playground.

"Hey, baldy!" a boy called out as he hopped off the swing set, waving at me and smiling.

I cringed, pulling my hair around my face self-consciously. I dreaded windy days, for it made it harder to keep my hair combed down around my face. "Leave me alone," I retorted, storming away.

"Whatever you say, baldy," the boy replied, laughing.

Tears burned my eyes as I sank onto the hard concrete, hoping the recess bell would soon ring. I hated feeling different and especially hated being taunted. Though I was thankful my accident had not left me with more devastating scars, I still desperately wanted to be normal just like the other children.

***

My parents were very active in the Mormon Church, and each morning before school, my three siblings and I trudged down to the church for a time of learning and prayer. I did not particularly understand or embrace everything I learned in the Mormon Church, but it was a way of life for my family — one we did not dare question. I pored over the Book of Mormon and the *Pearl of Great*

A LITTLE HELP FROM ABOVE

Price, trying to make sense of everything my teachers taught. I had many questions in my little mind, but it always seemed easier to just nod my head and participate in the lessons than to question the teachings of these books.

"Why can't you drink Coca Cola?" a little girl asked me at the lunch table one day as we pulled out our sack lunches.

I bit into my peanut butter sandwich and shrugged. "I'm Mormon. We can't have any caffeine. No soda pop, no chocolate, no tea."

The little girl wrinkled up her face and put her soda down. "Wow, you can't even have chocolate? That must be a bummer."

"I don't really think much about it," I replied. "I just do what they tell me to do and don't do the things I'm not supposed to do. We're taught that doing good works for the kingdom is the most important thing of all, so I try to be good and listen to my teachers." I had never really considered myself deprived because I didn't consume soda pop and chocolate and wondered why this little girl seemed so confused about my beliefs.

When I entered junior high, I was determined to be a hard worker. I obtained my first job at a Burger King, where I bussed tables after school. I enjoyed the meager paycheck I brought home and the satisfaction my duties brought me. I continued to do well in school and hold up a good front outside the home, wanting to please my parents and God, as I then knew him, more than anything.

One day, I came home from school and found my parents sitting across the kitchen table from my brother, looking quite angry.

"What's the matter?" I asked, slipping off my greasy fast food uniform. "Is something wrong?"

My mother looked up at me with tear-stained cheeks. "It seems your brother has gotten his girlfriend pregnant. How do you like that?"

I gulped. I had never known anyone in our church to do such a thing! "Really?" I squeaked, not knowing what else to say. My eyes strayed to my brother, who sat solemnly with his head bent down, obviously ashamed of what he had done.

"What will become of us now? The church will surely oust us if they find out what he's done," my mother moaned, wringing her hands in her lap.

My father cleared his throat and glared at my brother. "Surely this is not the Mormon way, son. You have shamed our family. Our lives will never be the same."

Our lives will never be the same? Fear gripped me as I slinked out of the kitchen and up to my room, where I sank onto my bed to process the news. My brother was a good person; surely the church would be able to see that and forgive him for what he had done. Surely this one incident would not haunt us forever.

While the church did not excommunicate my family, my parents were too ashamed to return. They feared everyone would look down upon our situation, and leaving seemed the best thing to do. I was greatly disturbed by the fact that we had to leave a place we called home for so many years.

I became bitter and angry after we left the church. I began to dabble in drugs, smoking cigarettes at first and slowly working my way up to marijuana. I didn't particularly enjoy smoking, but a part of me was secretly happy to rebel against the church that always imposed such strict and rigid guidelines upon my family.

When I was 15 years old, I got pregnant. Though we were not involved in our church at the time, my parents still held tightly to the Mormon beliefs and were once again shamed by their child's actions.

"There is only one thing to do," my father said sternly one night, sitting me down at the very same table he sat my brother down at not long before. "You must marry the boy."

Marry the boy? But I was only 15! I was a busser at a fast food restaurant, for heaven's sake. How on earth could I be married at such a young age, when I hadn't even completed high school? Tears burned my eyes as I placed my hands on my newly swelling belly, where new life brimmed within. I was going to be a mother and a wife at only 15 years old. Though I loved my boyfriend as much as a 15-year-old girl can love a person, I was sure I was too young for all this. I knew better than to go against my father's orders, however. I would marry the boy, and I would become a mother.

I gave birth to a beautiful little girl named Crystal shortly after I turned 16, and she grew to be the light of my life. I embraced my new role as a mother, awkwardly changing her diapers and feeding her as any new mother would. This was certainly not the life I imagined for myself, but I knew that somehow I would make it work.

When I was 18 years old, I had surgery to repair the remaining scars and the hairless side of my skull from my burn accident. As I lay in the recovery room, I wondered what my life might have been like if I had been blind and disfigured like the doctors predicted. I defied the odds and had gone on to live a very normal life after a very devastating event that should have scarred me for life. I was grateful I had been dealt a good hand, but it would be years later before I would come to understand the great God who had been looking over me, the God who had a wonderful future planned before me I could not yet see.

***

When I was 21 years old, my sister came to pay me a visit. We decided to go out to breakfast one morning to catch up on all life had dealt us in the past few months. My sister drove, and I buckled myself into the passenger seat, eager for our precious time together.

"Where do you want to eat?" my sister asked as we whizzed down the highway.

"Anywhere. Pancakes sound great. I'm starved," I replied. "Let me see how much cash I have on me." I leaned down and fumbled in my purse to check for loose change.

Suddenly, in the blink of an eye, the road spun before us. I heard a squealing and a terrible screeching of metal

A LITTLE HELP FROM ABOVE

on metal as two cars slammed into ours. I flew forward and hit my head on the dashboard and then again on the passenger side door handle. For a moment, everything went black, and I felt as though I could not breathe. "Uggghhh!" I moaned, while my head was whipped back against the seat. Instantly, pain shot through my entire body, and I felt myself go weak. "Help me ..." I murmured. "Help ..."

The next several moments were a complete blur — I drifted in and out of consciousness, trying to remain awake and aware of my surroundings. I knew this much: we had been in a terrible accident. I lay shivering on the seat, while my sister lay beside me, breathing heavily and sobbing.

Suddenly, out of nowhere, a man who I guessed to be in his early 30s was at my side, kneeling at my feet. "Miss, your teeth. Let me help you put your teeth back in."

My teeth? I felt my mouth and was shocked to discover all of my teeth had been knocked out of my mouth during my violent whiplash. "Oh, oh," I cried, tears springing to my eyes. "My teeth ..."

"There now, I'm going to help you put them back in. I need you to sit real still. If we act quickly, there will still be time to salvage them, and your smile will one day be as good as new. Hang in there, okay? You might feel a bit of pushing."

I clutched my side, reeling from the pain of the accident. I heard sirens blaring in the background and knew help had at last arrived. Though it had surely only been minutes, it felt like hours since the terrible crash. I felt as though I was in someone else's body, looking down on a girl lying on the front seat of a car in pain.

I winced as the kindly man gently pushed each tooth back into the socket of my gums, working quickly but methodically around my mouth. "There now, good as new. It looks like the paramedics are here. You're going to be just fine. I've got to get going because I'm late for a meeting. Good luck, miss."

The man stood; just as quickly as he had appeared, he was gone, vanished into thin air. I groggily pulled myself up in my seat and glanced around to the right and the left of me, looking for the man who saved my teeth. But he was nowhere to be found.

The next few hours were a whirlwind of activity, as I was hurried down to the local hospital and cared for. I suffered two black eyes and a broken nose, in addition to having all of my teeth knocked out. The doctors were amazed my injuries were not more extensive.

When the oral surgeon wheeled me into the operating room, he leaned down and shook his head in amazement. "You say that some man came alongside and put all your teeth back in your mouth?" he asked skeptically.

I nodded. "Yes. He was a … a guardian angel, I suppose. I don't know. He just came out of nowhere and disappeared just as quickly. I don't know if he was a dentist or a …" My voice trailed off as I began to wonder if, in my state of confusion, I imagined it all. How could a perfect stranger have known to come to my side and put my teeth in at that very moment? Was I crazy?

"A guardian angel." The surgeon chuckled. "You hear about those, you know. Guess it's possible. Call it what you want, but that man truly did save your teeth. After this surgery, you're most likely going to be as good as new. And you know what I'm going to use to glue those suckers back in?"

I shook my head. "No."

He grinned. "Hard as Nails. You know that super glue stuff? That should do the trick."

I furrowed my brow, confused. "Are you serious?"

He laughed. "No. Just wanted to get a good laugh out of you. Guess my joke fell flat. All right now, in just a few moments, you should be fast asleep, and when you wake up, you'll have that pretty smile back, okay?"

Nine hours later, I awoke, groggy and confused. "What … what happened?" I asked.

"Remember? Your teeth?" The surgeon was huddled over me, smiling. "Like I said, you should be back to normal as soon as you heal."

I felt for my swollen mouth and cringed. The accident began to replay itself in my mind. The screeching of the metal, my sister's scream, the car as it spun round and round before flying off the side of the road, the way my face hit the passenger door so hard it broke the handle … and that man … or that wonderful angel who had stopped alongside the road to help me. Who was he, and why had he come?

Hard Luck Kid. That was the term my father used to

describe me as a child. I survived the burn accident and now this one; surely someone was looking out for me. But was it possible God truly sent an angel to help me in my time of need?

After I recovered from my accident, I went to search for that mysterious man who helped me. I searched for a dentist office within miles of the scene of the accident, but there weren't any to be found. Dumbfounded, I began to truly believe God sent an angel to help me when I needed it most.

***

My life took a series of unexpected twists and turns during the next few years. I gave birth to another beautiful little girl, whom I named Marquise. My older daughter, Crystal, several years older than her, doted on her younger sister like she was a toy doll. The two became very close in the next few years, which pleased me greatly.

Meanwhile, however, my husband and I began to grow apart. He began to dabble with many inappropriate things, and we eventually separated. I was determined to make a good life for my girls and started working as a cocktail waitress in Las Vegas.

Eventually, I moved up to the position of bartender and found I enjoyed it immensely. I loved talking with the various customers who walked through the door of the bar and enjoyed the generous tips I received, as well. Though I longed to be home more with my girls, I knew there was no other work I could find where I could make such decent money for the hours I worked.

One evening, when I showed up for work, I heard several busboys whispering in a corner. "What's going on?" I asked nonchalantly, sauntering up to them.

One of the men looked at me with fear in his eyes. "Last night the bartender on duty was murdered. Right there where you're standing."

A chill went up my spine while I processed his words. "Murdered? You're kidding!" I knew Las Vegas had a high crime rate, but I never imagined someone would be murdered right here in my little bar. "I can't believe it," I muttered, shaking my head. "That's crazy."

"And true," the guy replied. "Good thing you had the night off."

"Yeah, good thing," I murmured, feeling suddenly uneasy. Once again, I was reminded of how close I came to death's door — and once again, I had been protected.

That night, as I walked to my car in the dark, empty parking lot, I glanced over my shoulder several times nervously, half expecting someone to jump out of the shadows and charge toward me. I knew many uniformed workers like myself were attacked during the wee hours of the night, and I feared now, more than ever, I might one day be one of them.

"Please, God, keep me safe," I prayed as I bolted for my car. I did not yet have a meaningful relationship with Jesus, but I was fairly certain it was God who had been watching over me all of these years, maybe even going so far as to send one of his angels down to earth to help me out. On this particular night, I was more than eager to get home to my girls and to the safety of our little home.

Life was not easy as a single mother. Though I continued to rely on the tips from my bartending job, I eventually found I could no longer afford my tiny apartment. My husband did not provide any income for my girls or me, leaving me with no choice but to send my daughters to my sister's house temporarily until I could get back on my feet. I did not want my girls to experience having to live out of a car. I prayed I could scrape up enough money in the future to provide a decent life for our family.

I eventually moved to Oregon, which seemed to offer a more family friendly environment for my children. I continued to work in the bars and raise my girls, all the while struggling with the typical single mom guilt that plagued me each night I left home to head to work. I was thankful that my older daughter, Crystal, had become like a surrogate mother to her younger sister and watched over her vigilantly. Despite their age difference, the two girls were quite close and continued to be so as they grew older.

We began attending a local Christian church where I met several kind people who seemed to have a genuine love for God. I was so taken aback by the way they embraced my girls and me, loving me without questioning my background or anything in my past. I had yet to develop a true relationship with Jesus. However, I knew I believed in God and that somehow, even though I had not always searched for him in my life, he had been searching for me, watching over me and waiting for me to come to him.

One Sunday morning, I awoke and decided to go skydiving on a whim. I had seen a local advertisement about a man who took people out skydiving in the local mountains. My husband had often told me I was not exciting, and somehow, I suddenly felt the urge to prove to him and everyone else that I truly was exciting. I could think of nothing more thrilling than jumping out of an airplane into midair!

"I don't think you should go," my older daughter told me over breakfast, twisting her mouth into a frown. "I just don't think it sounds very safe, Mom. I mean, skydiving? How about hiking a mountain? Wouldn't that be exciting?"

"Yeah, Mom, don't go," my younger daughter pleaded, throwing her arms around my neck. "Besides, we have church. We can't miss church."

I shook my head. "I know, I know, it's crazy, but I've always wanted to try this. I feel like if I don't go now, I'll never give it a shot."

My older daughter swallowed her cereal and stood. "Well, be safe, Mom. Please."

"I will, I promise." My stomach did a cartwheel at the prospect of actually embarking on such a journey. Surely it would be the adrenaline rush of a lifetime to jump from a plane!

My heart raced as I looked down out of the tiny plane at the dotted hills below me, replaying in my mind over and over what I was about to do. I was going to jump from a plane just minutes from now! What would it feel like as I descended? Would the air whip around me like a cape, or would it be perfectly still, as I'd always imagined it to be? I gulped hard and inched my way toward the opening of the plane.

"Ready to jump?" The instructor came to my side and adjusted my chutes. "You know what to do, right? You know when to deploy your chute as you descend?"

"Yup," I replied confidently. I was sure nothing would go wrong. After all, people did this sort of stuff every day.

"Okay, well on the count of five, the doors are going to open, and you're going to go on out, all right? Enjoy your trip down!"

I took a deep breath as the doors opened, a gust of air whipping at my face. Before I had much time to think, I was falling, slowly, slowly, slowly. *I'm doing it! I'm really skydiving! This is incredible!* I looked up at the sun, which seemed 10 times brighter from this high. The view before me was incredible, unlike anything I had ever seen from a plane. I was a bird, free and light as air, flying!

I pulled at my chute, but within seconds, I knew something had gone horribly wrong. I felt both chutes deploy at the same time, and they quickly became entangled as I descended at a more rapid speed toward the ground.

Panicked, I grabbed at the chutes, but it was impossible to detangle them from the position I was in. "God, help me!" I cried, or at least tried to cry. I looked down in horror at the ground before me, ready to swallow me up. I was going to die.

My mind flashed to the two accidents prior in my life. Someone had always been there to help me. This time, however, there was no one. It was just me and the air and my defective parachutes. I had no time to think, to pray, to figure things out. My life flashed before my eyes, and I thought of my two precious girls, who had adamantly begged me not to do this. *Oh, please, God, let me live! I need to raise my girls!*

These were the last words I thought before my body hit the ground with a thud.

As the world spun around me, I opened my eyes and found myself face to face with a strange man. "Am I alive?" I moaned.

"Yes, ma'am. Incredibly, you are. You landed on a hill here, and help is on the way. You're probably pretty banged up, but you're going to live, I believe. Just stay perfectly still until help arrives, all right?"

I blinked, unable to believe I was truly alive. How could I have survived such a fall? My foot was over my head, causing me to resemble a pretzel. Pain shot through my back like a bolt of lightning, and my leg hurt terribly. I knew I was in very bad shape, but I was thankful to be alive all the same. I blinked again, and to my surprise, the man who had just spoken to me was nowhere to be seen.

I lay back on the hard ground, my parachutes that had failed me billowing around me. Every inch of my body hurt, and my head thudded as I closed my eyes. "Oh, God, I'm alive! Thank you!" I groaned. I was still in shock. I knew I had once again defied the odds. Surely I should not have survived such a horrendous accident.

As it turned out, I broke my leg in eight places, my teeth and my back in three different places. I was put into a full body cast and spent the next several weeks resembling a plaster mummy. I lay on my couch in my tiny one-bedroom apartment, feeling helpless but oh so fortunate to be alive.

My mind raced back to the site where I landed and to the strange man who had appeared out of nowhere. Another guardian angel, perhaps? If that was so, God must surely be exhausted from having to work his angels so hard! Nevertheless, I was grateful for yet another chance at life. I knew God must have great plans for my life if he allowed me to live through so many horrific incidents.

My church graciously provided meals and babysitting for my girls during the next few weeks. Once again, I was touched by their love and generosity toward us. I was without words sometimes as perfect strangers entered my home and plopped down steaming hot casseroles onto my little kitchen table. I was getting just a taste of God's great love through these wonderful people.

I soon learned the man who owned the skydiving company had the highest fatality rate in the nation and several lawsuits had been taken up against him. I also learned I was the only person to ever survive such a horrific fall. This gave me all the more reason to believe God had truly carried me to the ground that nearly fateful morning.

During the time I was disabled in my confining body

cast, my truck was blown up when a man with ill intentions lit fireworks in it one night. I was devastated — it was one of my few meager possessions and also my sole source of transportation to work and church. To my utter disbelief, a group of people from my church showed up the next evening and picked up every piece of what was left of my truck.

Tears filled my eyes while I watched them stoop and crawl around the ground in the dirt, searching for remnants of my prized possession. I felt so undeserving of their selfless acts and yet so touched by their obvious love for me. Their kind acts left little room for me to feel sorry for myself in my body cast.

One afternoon, I met the woman who lived above me. She was a lovely woman who worked at the local grocery store across the street, and I often watched her as she walked home from work, whistling and smiling as she carried her bag of groceries. Though she led a simple life as a grocery bagger, she always seemed to be full of joy, as though she had just had the best day of her life. I often heard her call out "God bless you!" to people as she crossed the street.

"You're always smiling, always happy," I told her one day over tea. "What is that all about?"

She looked at me over her tea and smiled. "That, my dear, is called Jesus. He came into my life, and gave me a joy I thought I could never have. He gives me reason to smile each morning and to make the best of each day even when things don't seem so wonderful."

THE UNCHAINED

I thought about the past few weeks of my life, and how I had at times felt like I had nothing to live for. Though I was sure God had a plan for my life, I felt it hard to imagine life outside of the lonely, confined state I found myself in. Would this woman have smiled even through my situation? Somehow, I had a feeling she would have.

"I want that, too," I replied. "I grew up knowing about God, and I've been going to church recently. I really do feel God has been watching over me all my life, but now, sitting here, I really feel like there has to be more to all of this."

The woman squeezed my hand and smiled, tears filling her eyes. "Oh, Lori, there can be!" she cried. "All you have to do is pray and accept Jesus as your personal Savior, and you, too, can experience the joy I do each day! He will fill you with an inexplicable peace. Even when times get tough, you will know he has a plan and a purpose for you, and he will never forsake you. All you must do is acknowledge you are a sinner in need of a savior and ask him to come into your heart. Would you like to do that right now?"

I nodded eagerly, my heart beating quickly. "Yes, I would," I replied softly.

As the humble words tumbled from my mouth that morning, I felt an almost instant peace wash through my soul, as though I was becoming a new person right then and there. When I opened my eyes, I felt light as a feather, despite my heavy body cast. "Oh, that felt wonderful! I feel like the pieces of my life are all coming together!" I cried.

A LITTLE HELP FROM ABOVE

"I'm so happy for you, Lori," she replied. "God cares so much for you. Your life has just begun."

Suddenly, I found I could not stop smiling. Everywhere I went, I was filled with a joy that had been missing all those years. Slowly, I began to see just how much God loved me, and how, even when life seemed hopeless, he had really been there all along, watching over me and waiting for me to run into his arms.

My dear neighbor friend also led my older daughter in the sinner's prayer, and as my girls grew older, they developed their own personal relationship with Jesus Christ. I continued to attend church with the girls, thanking God each week for the loving and caring people who surrounded us. While I had grown up feeling like I had to serve God to get into heaven, I now understood serving God was something one wanted to do when they became a Christian, as a way of pleasing him rather than achieving salvation. I knew I was a sinner, of course, and I would stumble many times in my life, but just as he had plucked me from near death several times, he would also be there to pick me up when I fell again.

***

I spent many years as a single mother and continued to work as a bartender to make ends meet. I gained quite a reputation as the "Christian bartender who didn't drink." I enjoyed my job, however, and especially enjoyed the people I encountered on a daily basis. My job became my mission field, a place where I could talk to people each day who did not know Jesus and his amazing love. The church I am now attending, Evergreen Christian Center, didn't condemn me, but encouraged me in growing in my faith, praying with me for new employment.

One day, a handsome, tall man approached the counter and ordered a soda and a hamburger. I couldn't help but notice his large hands and even larger smile as I served up his order. We chatted briefly, and he left. He returned several days later, and then again. Each time, he ordered the same: a hamburger and a soda pop. We chatted more and more each time he came in, and I found myself drawn to him for some reason.

During one of our visits, this kindly man happened to mention he read his Bible every day.

"Are you a Christian, too?" I asked slowly.

He nodded, smiling. "I am. Are you as well?"

"Yes," I replied, smiling back. It was too good to be true! Not only was he handsome and sweet, but he loved the Lord as well.

Our brief conversations over hamburgers and soda led to a few dates, which eventually led to a marriage proposal. I was beyond thrilled to be engaged to my "Gentle Giant," as I affectionately referred to my fiancée. We spent hours poring over the Bible together, attending church together and just getting to know each other.

I learned he had been born with disabled legs, which forced him to wear leg braces as a child. He endured much teasing from cruel young children just like I had on the playground as a child. I was amazed at how God brought two people with so much in common together. We had an amazing bond, with the center of it being Jesus himself.

"How about saying our vows while skydiving?" my fiancée teased one night over dinner. "Wouldn't that be cool?"

"Hey, now," I replied, laughing, "somehow I don't think that would be a very good idea. I may have nine lives, but I'd like to keep a few of them, if you don't mind."

I set my fork down and thought for just a moment over the many times in my life God had watched over me, guarding me like a prized possession even when I did not yet know him well. "I am with thee always ..." I often felt the Lord say this to me in my life, whether it be through a whisper or a Bible verse or through a fleeting prayer. From a scared little 3-year-old girl to a down-and-out single mother to a newly engaged woman about to embark on the journey of a lifetime, my God had never left me or forsaken me, not even for a moment.

Skydiving, well, that seemed like an exciting adventure, but I hadn't a clue as I jumped from that plane living for Jesus would prove to be the most exciting adventure of all!

TRUST RESTORED
The Story of Rick
Written by Matt Norman

I watch the scenery out of my car window in excitement. I can recognize the houses now, even the trees. We're almost there — almost home. The last few weeks have been the worst ordeal of my young life, and all that has gotten me through are my memories of home and the hope that soon I would be back, back in my warm, familiar house with my loving mom and dad. Now, finally, I can relax.

I can see that Mr. Brown is relieved, too, now that he is about to be rid of us. It was clear from the beginning that my little sister and I weren't welcome in his home. If my parents intended our stay with them to be some kind of vacation, they made a big mistake. His children treated us as if we were less than human, and the Browns, for their part, had done nothing to discourage such behavior. I was hurt and confused the entire time. But now all that is forgotten. My only thoughts are of returning to the safety and love of my parents. And here we are!

Now Mr. Brown is pulling up to the curb in front of our house, and I'm ready to leap out and run to my beloved father's arms. But what I see as I get out makes me stop in my tracks. Who are these strange people I can see through our front window, moving about in our living room? What are our dining table, our sofa and chairs, even the bunk bed I share with my little sister doing in the

THE UNCHAINED

garage? Why have these strangers taken our pictures off the walls, and why are they replacing them with pictures of children I've never seen before? Most importantly, where are my mom and dad? So many questions are racing through my head, so many entangled emotions flooding my heart, I can only stand and stare, speechless. When I come to my senses and turn to ask Mr. Brown what is going on, he is gone.

He left our things on the curb and drove away. The strangers in our home carry our family portrait out of our house and toss it carelessly into the garage. Surely, they can see me, but they remain oblivious. It's as if I've been cut out from the world, a ghost. I am alone except for my 6-year-old little sister who keeps asking me questions that my 7-year-old self cannot begin to answer. I can only stand here wondering what has become of the world I know, what is to become of me, and what I have done to deserve this.

***

This was how we learned my parents were getting a divorce and our childhood home was no longer ours. After that, life would never be the same. In fact, even now on Sunday afternoons when the light is just right in the sky, I get a gnawing feeling in my stomach as the feelings from that day rush back to me.

TRUST RESTORED

***

"Kids, get your coats and shoes on; we have to get out of here. There's a bomb beneath the trailer."

I did as my Uncle Ron told me. I was ready to believe anything where he was concerned. Without pausing to wipe the sleep from my eyes, I leaped from bed and headed for the door. The first dim light had just broken on a cold, gray day, and a thin layer of ice covered the puddles in our driveway. My sister couldn't find her shoes, but we dashed out into the frigid darkness, anyway. Finally, cold and shivering, we got to the car and jumped in, huddling together for warmth. Some Christmas Eve this was turning out to be.

My aunt and her daughter were staying with us while our mother had surgery in the hospital. My mom would be getting home later that day, and I had been looking forward to a peaceful, happy family Christmas. I should have known better. As we sat in the car, tense and half expecting to hear an explosion, my uncle came out, leading my aunt. He went to the back end of the trailer and began groping beneath it, searching under the bedroom I shared with my sister. When he came up, he held a small cylindrical object with wires coming out of it. I was only a fourth grader, but I knew it was a pipe bomb.

Uncle Ron pulled out one of the wires, and we exhaled in relief. The bomb was disarmed. Then he led Aunt Rita over to the car, and we could see for the first time he was holding a large hunting knife to her side. The bomb was defused, but I realized with a sinking feeling the worst was yet to come.

After guiding Aunt Rita into the driver's seat, Uncle Ron got in the passenger side, placing the defused bomb on the floor at his feet. "Kids, we're going for a drive!" he informed us in a cheerful, chatty voice. "Your Aunt Rita will drive." We knew better than to protest.

Uncle Ron proceeded to give my aunt instructions. "Go out onto the highway, and be careful not to speed. We're going home. You should have known better than to stay away for so long, honey." He spoke calmly, as if nothing untoward or out of the ordinary was taking place. A veteran who learned to make bombs in the service, Ron always conducted himself as if he were still a soldier, his demeanor businesslike and impersonal. But we all knew that unpredictable violence was ready to explode at any time from beneath this placid exterior.

We drove for some time through the frozen, slate-grey morning, nobody making a sound. The world outside was silent, still and dark. I scanned the bleak horizon for signs of life but could find none. We were alone in the world and being led to an uncertain fate. Occasionally, my aunt or sister would stifle a sob, but nobody dared speak. We all knew it was necessary to maintain the illusion of normalcy for my uncle; we knew shattering that pretense would set him off.

"So, tell me, Rick, what would you like for Christmas?" my uncle asked, as casually as if we were sitting around the dinner table. We were now about halfway to his house, and still he held the knife into my aunt's side as she drove. My mind flashed back to the first time I'd been to his house, to help clean up behind one of his "episodes."

There were bullet holes through the television screen and riddling the walls, and the floors were smeared with blood. The blood, we would later learn, had come from Uncle Ron's wrists. Sometime later, we moved in with them. It was kind of a tense place to live, to say the least. Now I did my best to keep my composure, to keep from my voice anything that would break the casual air my uncle was trying to maintain.

"I'm hoping for a BB gun," I replied, and as I said so, I pictured myself using it right then to save my aunt, cousin and sister.

"Well," he replied, "I think I might have a pellet gun back at the house that would suit you just fine."

I noticed then my aunt was taking a route that went right through town, hoping someone would notice our plight and do something to help. I swallowed hard, thinking of what Ron might do when he caught on. I tried to distract him, expressing my enthusiasm about his pellet gun, but it was too late.

"Hey now, Rita, what are you trying to pull? You know better than to take this route. Now look what you've forced me to do," he said, and as he spoke, he grabbed me and pulled me into the front seat with him, pressing the blade against my throat. I could feel he had spent some time sharpening it. "You give her instructions now, Rick. Maybe she'll pay you more mind than she does me," my uncle said, still friendly. "Just make sure she doesn't speed!"

My uncle knew she wouldn't dare draw attention our way when my life was at stake. I trusted her, too. Nevertheless, with the knife snug against my throat, I asked her to do as my uncle said and slow down.

We made it through town without incident, but as we were pulling onto the highway, my aunt suddenly opened her door and bailed out onto the gravel shoulder of the onramp. I saw her face looking up at me, frightened and, it seemed to me, apologetic, as she hit the ground rolling. I couldn't help but feel I had been abandoned once again — this time, perhaps at the cost of my life.

The car rolled off the road and eventually came safely to a stop. By that time, my aunt was on her feet, running toward a nearby gas station. The knife blade felt as if it was burning a hole in my throat. My sister was screaming hysterically, sure I was about to be done in. I had sort of the same feeling myself. But then, without a word, my uncle let go of me, got out of the car and got into the driver's seat.

He disposed of the knife and bomb in a roadside bush and, still saying nothing and giving no indication that anything unusual had taken place, drove to the next exit where he turned around and headed back to pick up my aunt.

My aunt had already called the police, and when they showed up, I took them to where they could find the bomb and knife, thinking my uncle would be safely behind bars for some time to come. Soon after he was arrested, though, my aunt bailed him out and dropped all charges. She trusted him. As for my mother, my sister and me, from then on, we received threatening phone calls from him and had to have a regular police patrol go past our house. I was learning to trust nobody.

***

"So, kids, did you have fun at your great-grandpa's place?"

"Yes, Daddy," my sister and I both agreed as we climbed into our father's car. That we had answered without any enthusiasm seemed to escape my father's attention. He had such reverence for the old man it was secondary to him whether we'd enjoyed ourselves, as long as we'd spent time with him. I could understand his feelings. Our great-grandfather was well loved by everyone, and I felt similarly about him.

I didn't know what happened between my sister and great-grandfather, but in hindsight, I had a feeling that something had been wrong, that he had hurt her somehow. Even if I had known what was going on, I don't know how — at 10 years old — I would have approached my dad. He had problems of his own, problems I couldn't understand. But there were times I got the feeling, when he looked at me, the problems somehow traced back to me. His looks of love and affection were seldom unalloyed by a certain tinge of regret.

,r was a pastor by training, though now he
a convenience store. I couldn't have under-
the time, how deeply this fact pained him and
w. ay part in this was. It wasn't until years later I
learned the true story — he had been a widely sought after
pastor in the years before I was born, and he had lost his
prestigious position after my mother became pregnant
with me for the simple fact that he and my mother were
not yet married at the time.

While my father went on to pastor at smaller congre-
gations, he never recovered from the fall he had taken and
the role the church played in it. He had become an alcoholic and lost his latest post as a pastor because of it. Now
it was clear to all he was haunted by the regrets of his past.
Still, to me, he was the world.

***

Never forget that it's a mistake to have faith in anyone,
including yourself, I told myself. My great-grandfather
had been the patriarch of our entire family, someone everybody looked up to. I couldn't help but feel the same, ad-
miring his graceful presence. It wasn't until years after his
death that I learned the whole truth — he had been mo-
lesting every young girl in our family for three genera-
tions. I couldn't contain the anger that filled me when I
learned this, and had he still been alive, I'm not sure what
I would have done to him. But once the anger passed,
there was only a deep sense of betrayal.

TRUST RESTORED

I felt like all of the wonderful memories I had of him, of times with the family at his house, were based on a mountain of lies. My grandparents and the rest of my family who knew the truth had been covering for him for years, keeping my aunts, my cousins and my sister, all those who had been irreparably damaged by the man, from speaking out. It was another reminder that nothing was what it seemed, and nothing stays true.

***

"Rick, I know I tell you this all the time, but you sure do have a good hand with those horses. After you ride them, they're calm for the rest of the day. I don't know what I'd do without you."

I beamed. Compliments from Dr. Roberts always made me feel proud. It wasn't just that he was a world-renowned doctor and health advisor to the royal families of several nations, or that he was one of the best-known and respected figures in the entire city. It wasn't even the kindness and generosity he had shown my father and the new life he provided for us — a beautiful home and 2 acres of land on his beautiful ranch in the city's nicest suburb, simply in exchange for caring for his horses and house-keeping his mansion whenever he was away. What really made it special was I trusted him. He had taken an interest in me and treated me as if I was not only a human being, but a special person. And I could feel it was out of genuine care and affection.

THE UNCHAINED

"Thanks, Dr. Roberts, I do my best."

"Hey, Rick, I'm getting tired of this. How many times do I have to tell you, call me Mark."

"Yes, Dr. Roberts. I mean, Mark."

"That's a boy. By the way, it sounds like you're coming down with something. How's your throat?"

"It is a little sore today. No big deal, though."

"Nonsense, you don't want it to turn into anything serious. Why don't we go down to my office? I have some things that will have you feeling good as new."

"That's really not necessary, sir. Er, Mark."

"Consider it an order, Rick. I'll meet you at my car in a few minutes."

As I ran in and washed up, I marveled for the hundredth time at the care Dr. Roberts was showing my family and me, in particular. I had gone from being an invisible boy, standing on a street corner with no home, to being like a son to this world-famous and universally esteemed man.

Some time earlier, my sister and I had gone to live with our father in the inner city. There, my junior high school had been more dangerous than an evening with my Uncle Ron. Then Dr. Roberts had come into our lives. Since then, things had been peaceful and pleasant in a way I hadn't experienced since before my parents' divorce. All in all, everything was looking up for us, all thanks to Dr. Roberts. And now, I was riding in his shiny new Mercedes Benz convertible through the city.

It was after hours, and his office was closed, so he took

me through the back door. He checked his phone messages. There were dozens of people with a myriad of ailments either inveighing Dr. Roberts to save them or thanking him for miraculous cures already affected. I was reminded once again I wasn't the only one who placed a deep faith in him. So there was nothing that could have prepared me for what I was to discover firsthand that day. The great Dr. Roberts was a child molester.

It only happened once, and since then, I'd been able to repress the memory of the molestation itself. What I couldn't forget was the feeling of betrayal. Once again, my trust had been cruelly broken. Another father figure let me down. And this time, there was no one who could help me. Dr. Roberts was a pillar of the community, and were I to accuse him, surely nobody would believe me. I didn't even dare tell my father. In fact, it now occurred to me, maybe that was what hurt more than anything — the fact that I couldn't tell my father.

***

"Man, what are you talking about? You're the luckiest guy I know. You might be the luckiest guy on earth. You're loaded. Everybody loves you; you have a million friends. And, oh yeah, I've never seen you with less than a quarter pound of cocaine in that freezer bag you carry around," I replied. "What do you have to be upset about?" But Fred just shook his head, slowly and despondently.

"I know all that. My life is a bowl full of cherries. I

make $100,000 a year just driving back and forth from one city to another. I've got no problems. Not a worry in the world. I've got it made. So, tell me, why am I so miserable? Why do I feel my life is worth nothing, that I'd be better off dead?"

I didn't know what to say to this. I could see the utter despair in Fred's eyes, could feel the pain in his voice. Even though I envied him his job moving cocaine from San Francisco to Kansas City, I knew he was in real need of help. And I really wanted to tell him something that would make him feel better. I searched my heart. There had to be some good news I could give him. But I found nothing. And I realized it was because, inside, I felt just the same as he did. Only I wasn't as honest with myself about it.

On the surface, my life, too, seemed to be a bowl of cherries. I had a fast car, my own apartment and no problems to bother me. I also had a great group of friends — friends who I knew would have my back in any situation. I trusted them like I hadn't trusted anyone in a long time. This was true of two in particular, brothers and leaders of a biker gang. The two had taken me in like a third brother.

Besides being loyal, they were also exciting to be around. Between the two of them, they had been shot twice and stabbed a dozen times, including some wounds inflicted on each other. Nights with them and their friends often ended with us riding through town, armed with pistols and baseball bats, seeking revenge for a drive-by shooting or an assault on one of our own.

TRUST RESTORED

Then there were my friends from work, mostly college students. They were just as fun, in their own way. Nights with them often ended in a brawl with random groups we encountered, followed by drunken drives home. On one occasion, I drove through the night without being conscious of it, only coming to awareness with the dawn. By then, I was in the middle of nowhere, hours away from my home.

With all of this excitement, why was I still so unhappy? Why was I continually haunted by the feeling that I lacked something and driven to take greater and greater risks with my life? I looked up at Fred, apologetically.

"I wish there was something I could tell you to make you feel better, Fred." But there wasn't. I was empty.

More than once, during those days, I had been on the edge of suicide. I'd come so far since then, and yet in the dead of the night, I was occasionally still prey to the same doubts and anguishes.

Back then, I fooled myself by running from the truth, always keeping myself distracted from the doubt gnawing away at my insides. Was I only doing the same thing now? If I had really changed since then, how could these memories still unnerve me so? Had I ever really escaped that blackness?

It started as a slight queasiness, barely even noticeable. I shrugged it off as a result of the bottle of beer I'd just drank and turned my attention back to the conversation going on between my friends. Then I began to see dark red at the periphery of my vision. I watched with detached curiosity as it slowly spread over my field of sight until I could barely see anything. Moments later, everything was black. At this point, it occurred to me something was definitely wrong. I leapt from my seat, holding my hands to my eyes. Only then did I notice the numbness that started spreading through my extremities, starting at my hands and feet and moving through my arms and legs. In another instant, I collapsed.

"He's turning blue! Does anyone know CPR?"

"Somebody do something!"

Lying on the floor, helpless to get up, I heard my friends' cries of concern. It sounded as if their voices were crossing an enormous gulf to reach me. Then that, too, faded, and I was alone in a world of blackness. I felt my eyes were open, and I was looking into an infinite sea of black. I then came to understand I was moving through this pitch darkness, being pulled farther into it by some inexorable force. I could even see my destination — the center of all the blackness, a point somehow different than the pure black around me. Only then did I start to feel terror. I knew somehow I didn't want to go where I was being taken, that once I reached that spot, there would be no coming back and no future for me.

With all my might, I fought to remain where I was. With no arms and legs to pull with, and with nothing even to pull against, I concentrated every last bit of my will on somehow arresting my progress. Nothing happened. I crept ever deeper into the black. Still, I strained with all of my might until I felt whatever was left of me would explode from the effort. And suddenly, somehow, my movement stopped. The instant it did, I felt myself falling toward earth, and I opened my eyes. I could see the familiar faces of my friends, relieved to see me return to consciousness. I was completely drained from the exertion of pulling myself back.

***

I was, as usual, not very happy. But I was doing my best to distract myself from that. A friend and I were working on our motorcycles. He was telling me something, some story. Then suddenly, without warning, I was looking at myself. I was standing on the other side of the room, and I could see myself clearly — could see where I really was, standing near my friend. He had gone on talking and I, for my part, looked normal. I was listening, even smiling. Only I wasn't there, just my body. My real self, my awareness, was across the room, watching. I was free from my body, and the feeling was indescribable.

All the worry, anger and doubt that burdened my body, that made my young life so consistently unhappy, vanished. Through no doing of my own, it had been removed, and in its place was a feeling of lightness. It felt as if I'd lived my entire life in chains and was tasting freedom for the first time. The weight of the world had been lifted from my shoulders, and after years of being oppressed by doubt and fear, I finally knew peace.

Though the whole experience lasted only a few seconds, the event and the feelings it brought were as powerful to me as any other memory I possessed. Yet, it hadn't been until years later, after I had run away from my dissolute and self-destructive past to seek something more meaningful, that I bothered to compare the experience with the dark one that came later in my life.

In both cases, I left my body and felt a sense of peace, of relief from the burdens of my day-to-day existence. But the other feelings each instance brought were polar opposites. Where one had been pure freedom, the other had seen the initial feeling of peace replaced by intense terror, as I was filled with the certain knowledge that only misery awaited me.

At the time, I couldn't face what that second experience meant. But I knew I never wanted that experience again, and I began to question myself and my way of life. It would be years before I started to find answers, and now, those answers felt empty.

My mother indoctrinated the practice of prayer into me from a very young age, and for much of my youth, it was a frequent occurrence. Prayer had become a habit, a part of my life, but I had long ago stopped expecting an answer to my prayers. It was just another formality required on the road to heaven, akin to the public declarations of faith my church required in my youth. Still, in moments of despair like this one, I rekindled my youthful hope that if I just prayed hard enough, I would finally get my answer.

I knelt by my bed and cast my thoughts heavenward,

asking that things be made the way I wanted them to be. I threw every bit of the rancor I was feeling into my words, willing them to be heard and heeded. I prayed this way for at least an hour, but eventually, I had to admit it felt as if I was talking to myself. I broke down, feeling crushed.

"What is wanted of me? I can't try any harder to make things work. I can't do everything all by myself. Why is there no help for me anywhere I turn? This is too much for me. I give up."

It was at that moment I suddenly felt something, a feeling I had been hungry for without knowing it — a feeling I had known before but had forgotten existed. I had thrown myself from the highest cliff in utter despair only to be caught by a cloud, gathered up into infinite softness and told to rest there, assured that everything would be fine. I felt as if I was floating, soaring above the world and looking down on it, and knowing with a full heart that all was as it should be. I had surrendered, thrown myself into the arms of the Lord — and to my astonishment, he caught me!

All of my life, every time I let myself depend on something or someone, every time I trusted someone, I had been cruelly let down. But I had never completely given my trust to Christ. Until now, that is. And here, as the aching emptiness inside me filled with warmth and love, I knew that was the one thing I needed to do.

The moment I finally let myself be saved, rather than trying to save myself, had been a time of great joy. I realized, for the first time, what a turning point that had been.

THE UNCHAINED

After that, after I stopped trying to force things and started to let faith guide me, so much good came into my life — my wife and children, so many good and true friends, better relationships with my family. It hadn't all been good, of course. I had needed, and taken, all the help I could get from the local church, where so many people understood just what I was going through.

There was so much in my past to foster mistrust, to make it second nature. It always seemed there was nothing I could count on, nothing important to me that couldn't be taken away, without warning. And I was still subject to that fear. But looked at as a whole, my past told a different story. I moved 46 times, attended 13 different schools and had been let down at every turn, until my life seemed like a cruel joke at times. And yet, through all the changes and broken hearts, something had been guiding me, helping me when I was on the brink and pushing me slowly toward the salvation I needed. Trust came hard for me, but again and again, God came through for me.

***

"Rick, you're crazy. If you take us in there any farther, we'll all be drowned. You do what you want, but I'm heading back now before the tide comes in."

Karen, my wife's cousin, looked around at the rest of the group to see if she was the only one who felt that way.

"Yeah, I'm with you, Karen. I don't know if this whole thing is such a good idea."

TRUST RESTORED

But the rest of us weren't ready to turn back. The beauty of the caves sheltered beneath the ocean side cliffs and only exposed during low tide enthralled all of us. As we went along the ocean side, jutting cliffs would bar our way. We would have to wait for the tide to recede and expose enough beach for us to pass around the cliffs and reach the next strip of safe beach. There, we would wait for the tide to recede further, allowing passage around the next cliff. While it was exciting and rewarding, it was also dangerous.

If the tide came in and made a cliff impassable after we had gone past it, we would be trapped against the cliff walls, forced to climb the steep and jagged rocks to avoid being drowned by the waves. There were some points where our safe waiting place consisted of a small cave, which was being continually beaten by the ocean and where any escape from rising waves would be impossible. There had been many Coast Guard rescues in similar places along the coast.

Nonetheless, I had made the trip before and timed everything according to the tides to give us a wide margin of error for a safe return, without even having to get wet. So as Karen went back to the seaside cabin we all were sharing, the rest of us pressed on. Soon, though, we came to the most precarious point yet.

"Rick, sorry to say it, but Karen's right. I'm getting out of here while the getting's good. Anyone else?" And so our party lost three more.

Things became more frightening as we went farther

from the safety of retreat and reached the most difficult juncture of all. We were on a small patch of sand with sheer cliff walls to one side and the crashing surf on the other. The waves could be deceiving, sometimes appearing to be growing, only to recede momentarily and then appear to grow again. Now it looked as if they were growing; if it continued, our way back would be blocked by the violent waves. Then it would only be a matter of time before the waves crushed us against the cliff face.

To make matters worse, there was no safe area visible around the cliff in front of us. To proceed would mean putting absolute trust in me. "Come on, Rick, if we don't turn back now, we'll need to be rescued. If we survive, that is. Why don't we all just go back now? We've come far enough."

Despite appearances to the contrary, I knew the tide was receding according to schedule. Only three were willing to take the leap of faith. When we cleared the last cliff, the ocean seemingly fell away and opened up into a breathtakingly beautiful tidal pool. We were alone, and because the ocean was so far away on this beach, everything was now calm and peaceful.

I looked again at my three companions — my wife and our two children. Of the 12 who set out, only they had the trust in me to continue on. And I thought to myself how fitting a metaphor it was for life. We who had trust had been rewarded with this paradise. I looked around at the serene setting and the three people I loved most in the world. *Thank you Jesus*, I thought. *You've shown me the way through all the dark passages to this perfect moment.*

I shook my head in disbelief. I, who had once been so unable to trust anyone or anything, now held the complete trust of these precious people, all because I learned to place my life in the hands of the Lord. Not everything has been easy since I learned this trust. I suffered a debilitating back injury that cut short a promising career and had me in bed for three years. Even now, 10 years and two major surgeries later, the pain is often unbearable, and I will never be able to return to my former work.

Now I understand why God sent Moses to the desert. Moses was too headstrong and would not listen to God — he needed to be humbled and become a father to understand God a bit more. But most of all, God had to tear down the old and rebuild from the bottom up. The tearing hurts like crazy, and the building takes time and dedication.

For several years, my losses crushed me. I was convinced I was a failure, unable to provide for my family. I was certain they had lost all respect for me, and believe me, that pain was far greater than any physical pain I endured. I gave up on life, lost interest in everything and felt stripped of all I valued — I felt utterly powerless.

And that is when God truly took hold of me. I realized that I — on my own — truly am powerless and always have been. The only strength is through God. But that strength is limitless.

I know there will always be events old and new to haunt me and challenge my trust. But I also know I will hold onto my faith, no matter how great the test. Trusting in Christ, putting one's life completely in his hands, isn't always easy. But it is always worth it!

HIDDEN TREASURE
The Story of Doreen
Written by Eric Ayala

Maturation from teenaged girl to woman can be harrowing under the best of circumstances. Hormonal changes in my body were accompanied with bouts of severe depression. I thought about dying a lot, and I began cutting my arms and wrists with razors. Not enough to kill myself; just enough to hurt. It was a very mournful and brooding period in my life, and I expressed those emotions with poetry on the pages of a journal.

Crippling fears — silent tears wash over my tattered self-image. Abuse — misuse — distrust; I have become my own worst enemy. Broken — no one to help me — no one to fix me — no one to love me. Cries echo throughout infinity; prayers go unanswered. Can anyone hear me? Does anyone care? I'm drowning. I can almost taste the sweet release of death.

My family never noticed and didn't seem to care much. I covered my cuts with long sleeves and bandages, but there was no camouflage for the pain.

I attended Sunday school and confirmation classes at a Lutheran church in our neighborhood. But we never attended regularly — we were among the "holiday only" churchgoers. My dad's father was a Lutheran minister, and my dad felt he had so much church growing up that he didn't need to go anymore.

But to me, the church represented some semblance of

solace. I found myself there a lot at night when no one was around. I'd go to the altar and kneel and cry and then return home to the same cycle of shameful mutilation.

My mother already had two sons from a previous marriage when she met my dad. In August 1952, I came along, nine months into their union. Initially, I was the perfect child in my father's eyes — I quickly learned that perfection is fleeting. By the time my sister, Janice, was born, my blond-haired, blue-eyed star had lost its luster. At 8 years old, I'd become pretty much nonexistent to him. I tried desperately to regain his favor. Nothing I did was good enough, so I started acting out to get attention.

We lived in a four-bedroom, one-bathroom house in the middle of suburbia. Keeping a messy room was a cardinal sin growing up. My father was a stern man with a lot of rules. He was also a very angry man. After he was born, he was left on the doorstep of an orphanage. Even though he was adopted and raised by two wonderful people, he never forgave his biological parents for what they'd done to him. The discovery of his mean streak put an abrupt end to my mischievous antics. Any perceived disobedience warranted a beating. My brothers had become accustomed to his dictatorial disposition; as I grew older, so did I.

Goofing off and not paying attention in class and failing grades were sure to garner a firm parental hand. I was given notices by my teacher to bring home, but there was no way I could let my parents get a hold of them, so I forged my mother's signature. Naturally, I was grounded when they found out. A month may as well have been perpetuity. At the tender age of 14, my entire life flashed before my eyes.

"Doreen, it's April. Can you talk?"

"Yes, but not long."

"Are your parents still making you stay in the house for what you did?"

"Yes." I rolled my eyes and pouted as I glanced across the family room at my dad lounging in his favorite chair, buried behind a wall of newspaper.

"A bunch of us are going down to the diner for sodas and to listen to the new Elvis Presley album. Can you come?"

"You know I can't."

"Zach will be there."

Zachary Morgan was the cutest boy in our class. He was the epitome of sixth grade cool. Where he went, all the girls wanted to follow. It was killing me to be stuck at home. I pulled into a corner of the room, a safe distance from my father so as not to be overheard.

"What time are you going?"

"In about 15 minutes."

"I'll meet you at the corner."

"But, I thought …"

"I'll be there; just wait for me."

I hung up the phone and nonchalantly slipped upstairs to my room to change into something I thought would impress Zach. Just as I opened the window and started to climb out, my bedroom door swung open. I turned sharply and stared into my father's stoic visage.

THE UNCHAINED

"Just where do you think you're going?"

"I — I — I was …"

Caught red-handed and red-faced — between imprisonment and empowerment — I struggled to come up with a plausible explanation. Before I could do or say anything more, he charged in and snatched me away from the window. He hit me so hard I went flying across the room, and I bounced off the wall and onto the bed. Picking me up, he smacked me again, and I flung headlong into the opposite wall. He then pulled my pants down and spanked me. It was absolutely horrifying. I'd never been treated so brutally before. After that, I walked around on eggshells, almost afraid to breathe in his direction — obeying more out of fear than respect.

A few days later, as I started home from school for lunch, I realized I was in such a rush that morning, I hadn't made my bed. I knew what would be waiting for me. As I bolted through the door toward the kitchen, my cover story had already taken shape. We only lived a couple of blocks from school, and I ran all the way so as to appear flustered and disheveled. I startled my mother who was standing at the counter making sandwiches.

"Doreen, what on earth?"

"There was a man," I panted. "He tried — he tried to grab me."

"What?"

"I fought him off, and I ran."

She rushed to my side and eased me down in a chair. Her concern was genuine. My guilt at having lied was palpable, but I couldn't run the risk of being beaten because of an innocent oversight.

"Are you all right?" She poured me a glass of water.

I nodded.

"I'm calling the police."

My mouth dropped. I didn't want it to go this far, but the train was in motion, and if I got off now, I'd be run over. When the police arrived, I described the man and the car he drove in painstaking detail. How afraid do you have to be in order to make up something so terrible?

A Lie Realized

At the age of 15, my girlfriend and I were walking down the street a week later when a swarthy-looking man drove up alongside us. He called me over. I thought he wanted directions. He was saying something I couldn't make out, but I saw he had his pants down, and he was fondling himself. I was mortified. We turned and ran away screaming. I could see my house from the corner, and my dad was standing in the yard. He dashed toward us, and we jumped in his car and sped after the man — we didn't catch him. My dad immediately drove to the police station to file a report. I was hysterical and shaking as I realized that a lie I'd constructed had actually become reality.

"Look at the way you're dressed. You look like a whore," was the first thing my mother said to me when we arrived home. It was quite a different reaction than I expected. It just didn't make sense based on how she'd responded before. I had on a simple knit dress; there was nothing sensual or salacious about it. They made me feel worse by putting the blame for what happened on me. My mom then did something unexpected and called the pharmacist to get me Valium. These were the days when no prescription was necessary. The answer to just about every horrible ordeal life threw your way could be found in a pill bottle or at the bottom of a liquor bottle.

My dad drank a lot, but he was what is commonly known as a functioning alcoholic. He controlled his drinking for the most part with the understanding that he had to work to support the family.

A year later, the man who accosted me was caught, and I had to identify him, which brought up all those horrible things again. The nightmare continued to haunt me, but the beatings had come to an end. My parents chose instead to ground me. Given the failure of my last escape attempt, I willfully complied.

The Wonder Years

In the summer of 1966, I again found myself distraught, contrite and crying at the altar of the church, when I saw what seemed to be a cloudy, ghostlike ethereal mass. It had no shape or form, and I blinked away the tears to make sure I wasn't seeing things. Was it a man? Was it the minister? I froze in fear.

"Doreen, I will always take care of you."

The voice was so clear. My panic resolved into an incredible sense of calm and wonderment. It couldn't have been my imagination. I felt this must be the Lord. I had no real connection to the church. I was never taught about such things, and I didn't know much about the Bible. With the exception of some rehearsed litany we recited in Sunday school, that was the extent of it.

The peace that came over me only lasted for a moment. Life as I knew it didn't change much. I was still depressed, but the experience lingered long after the feeling was gone. I hid the words he spoke deep in the recesses of my heart like buried treasure. The cutting eventually stopped, but just like any other addiction, a replacement was just around the corner.

I had my first taste of alcohol between my junior and senior years of high school. We had a pool in our backyard, so I invited friends to my house while my parents were out of town. We swam and had a good time just hanging out. It was very esoteric by today's standards. There were no drugs. There was no sex. Nothing untoward was going on until some of the guys started getting restless.

"Hey, Doreen," one of the boys hanging close to Zach yelled, "does your dad have any beer in the refrigerator?"

I suddenly realized that soda and potato chips weren't going to be enough for them. There was beer in the refrigerator, and there was some alcohol, but I didn't dare get into it. It was too obvious an infraction to try and cover up. I didn't want the fun to stop and appearing uncool was not an option, so I brought out the libations to keep the party going.

There was no more drinking for me until after I graduated high school. I suppose I inherited my father's tolerance and propensity for alcohol. It almost came naturally to me, as if it were a part of growing up or a rite of passage. Drinking and parties became a routine that soon started growing increasingly out of control.

I'd taken a job at a savings and loan and befriended another teller. She invited me to her house for a party, and that's when I met him. Harold was from a farming family. He'd quit school in the ninth grade to help his dad out. I didn't really care about all that. He was attentive and fun — he made me laugh. He was nice to me, and that's all that mattered. I just wanted somebody to love me, and I wanted to love him back. That was more than I was getting at home. My parents didn't approve, and that didn't faze me in the least. Harold and I dated over the next several months and made plans to be married the following June.

"Your father and I aren't coming," my mother announced with the proper amount of disdain in her voice.

"I don't care," I rebuffed. "We're still getting married."

"Doreen, how can you marry a man who is not of our caliber?"

"Our caliber? Mother, are you saying that we're better than them just because his family lives on a farm?"

She didn't answer. The look in her eyes spoke volumes. I shook my head, stood up from the kitchen table and started toward the door. "We're getting married this Saturday. If you guys want to come, you're welcome."

Despite their bravado, they both came around. My mom actually put together a very nice reception at the house with only three days' notice. I guess she figured this was a fight she was not going to win. She wasn't going to get her way. I was going to marry Harold no matter what.

We were married in a little country church in Hampshire, Illinois (neither of us were members — the pastor just allowed us to marry there.) I got pregnant soon after the wedding. Matthew was born the following year. There I was — barely 20 years old, married and a mother. It was hard. I was trying to live up to what I thought marriage was supposed to be. We should have been living in a house not an apartment. My parents owned their own home, and I wanted to raise my family in that kind of security. Neither Harold nor I were ready for the responsibility of what it meant to be a husband and wife, let alone parents.

Borrowing money from my grandfather, we were able to put a down payment on a three-bedroom house. However, we really couldn't afford the payments. My dad got Harold a job doing landscaping with his company. Then, before I knew it, he was taking classes at a trade school to become an electrician. But he really wasn't suited for that. He wasn't happy, and neither was I. We both turned to the only source of comfort we had come to know. Drinking only underscored our unhappiness, which was intensified when we fought.

"I'm doing the best I can do, Doreen. What else do you want from me?"

THE UNCHAINED

"You're smart. Why can't you change?"

"I don't need to change, and I don't want to change."

Harold was a simple man with simple dreams. He didn't seem to have any ambition, a quality that I'd grown to dislike. He was reared very differently than I was. He had a huge family. On Sundays, all the aunts, uncles and cousins would gather at Grandma's house for dinner, which was unlike my family, who only came together on holidays. They'd laugh together and play — they really seemed to love each other. All the kids ran around outside while the women busied themselves in the kitchen, and the men hunkered down around the television for whatever sporting event they fancied. It was all very foreign to me — very Norman Rockwell and strangely comforting at the same time. Still, settling for the life of a farmer was not what I wanted for me or my son.

I turned to my mother, "Mom, what am I going to do? I just hate to be around him when he's drinking. I don't want Matthew to be around him, either."

"You don't have to stay with him, Doreen. We'll loan you the money to get a divorce."

Loan? It wasn't as if I could pay them back. I was stunned. She didn't want us to get married in the first place, and now, here she was, offering support for a divorce.

"Okay, if that's what you think I should do."

Matthew was 1 1/2 when we finally called it quits. There was no trying to fix anything. Harold was devastated; yet, he went along with it as if he had no say in the matter at all. I just listened to my mother because that's what I was programmed to do. In many ways, I was still the same little girl who grew up trying to please them in order to get their attention. If I didn't do what I was told, I was disciplined for it. Walking away from Harold, I could almost hear my mother gloat, "See, I told you so." She had won after all.

Harold moved out. I remained in the house with Matthew. I was unbelievably lonely. To satiate my desire, I took a job at a really nice bar and subsequently began doing something I had not sought out to do, something of which I was not at all proud — I began dating married men.

A wife of a man that I'd been seeing for a while caught wind of our affair. She knew me from the bar because she'd come in with him on occasion, and she somehow got the phone number to my parents' house and called.

"Hello."

"This is *Mrs.* Bixby."

"Who?"

"I'm the wife of the man your slut of a daughter is having an affair with, and if you don't keep her away from him, I'm going to kill her! Do you understand me?"

My mom was so freaked out she immediately called me at work to warn me. That was enough of a wakeup call for me. I ended it.

Unable to pay the mortgage on the house, it was eventually repossessed. With no place to go, Matthew and I moved back in with my parents. I didn't want to be back under their scrutinizing eyes, so in a matter of weeks, I decided to pack up everything that would fit in my car. A girlfriend of mine, who was divorced and had a 2-year-old son, and I were on our way to Oregon.

Once again, I found myself in the dubious position of hurting Harold. I felt so guilty. Not only had I left him high and dry, I was going to move his son across the country, which would essentially bring an end to whatever bond they could have had. He wasn't the best father, and he really didn't know what he was doing, but neither did I. It was one of my biggest regrets.

Tearfully, we sat on the front step of my parents' house and watched Matthew playing in the yard.

"Oregon?" he asked. "Why do you have to go so far away?"

"My brother, Randy, and his wife are there. They're family."

"What about Matt? He's my family. He's my son."

"Then you'll have to come visit him there."

"You're taking away the one good thing I have in my life. Why are you doing this, Doreen?"

"Because I have to," I replied, but I couldn't look at him.

I couldn't bear to see the hurt in his eyes. As he swept Matthew up in his arms to say goodbye, I turned away in tears.

HIDDEN TREASURE

New Life, Same Doreen

Hillsboro was only a few miles away from Portland. I thought here was my chance to start fresh, leaving all the shackles of the past behind and taking life by the horns. The Pacific Northwest offered new horizons — new adventures. My girlfriend and I only stayed with my brother for a few days before we got our own apartment in Beaverton.

Neither of us was able to find a job right away, so we applied for public assistance and food stamps; the state paid for childcare. Business college seemed a viable alternative while waiting for the right job opportunity. Most days, after dropping the kids off at daycare, we foolishly opted to frequent the bars and drink; at the end of the day, we'd pick them up and go home.

Habits like smoking pot and snorting cocaine seemed to enhance the nights we spent at the bars. I'd sometimes bring guys home, still hoping to find the right one. But all this left a dark, vacuous hole in my soul.

Heavily intoxicated, I walked home from one of my favorite haunts at 1 a.m. on a hot, sultry night in 1974. It had been a long day, and my feet were hurting, so I kicked off my shoes and carried them. All I wanted to do was take a shower and lay under a cool air conditioner. Two guys drove up next to me and offered a ride. In my condition, I didn't think anything of it. It seemed pointless to keep walking. Besides, I knew Pete from the bar. There were no red flags, no sign of imminent danger, but instead of taking me home, we ended up at an old house that appeared to be abandoned.

"What are we doing here, guys?" I was trying not to sound alarmed.

"Relax," Pete slurred as he put the car in park and ran his hand over my thigh. "We just wanna have a couple of beers and a little fun, that's all."

I didn't like the odds. I didn't like the feeling that was creeping up on me, either. If I ran, where would I go? We went into the house and staggered down the stairs to the basement. It was damp and cold. I felt suffocated. The two of them looked at each other as if they shared a secret to which I wasn't privy. Wiping their mouths like hungry lions about to devour their prey, Pete pulled at me and forced me down on the ground.

"Shhh, I'm not gonna hurt you."

He forced himself on me, and I couldn't do anything to stop him. Once he was done, the other man took his turn. Trembling — crying — I was completely demoralized.

Because I was drunk, I must have deserved it. I was too ashamed to report the attack to the police. Emotionally broken, I ended up in the hospital for about a week. From that moment on, I've been unable to go into a basement without reliving the humiliation of that night. You would have thought something so debasing would have soured me from the very taste of alcohol; the truth is, though it was a horrifying bump in the road, it only slowed me down for a time.

I met Jack in a bar over the Memorial Day holiday in

HIDDEN TREASURE

1975. He moved in with me the day after. He liked me, and he was wonderful with Matthew. Jack was good-looking, funny and smart. He was everything you could want in a man, except he didn't have a job. I should have known. I thought he was what I'd been looking for to fill the need and emptiness in my life. We partied, smoked pot and drank, and drank, and drank. Sex was great. He even wanted more kids.

Impetuously, we were married by the justice of the peace at the local courthouse that same year. Afterward, to celebrate with friends, we went to a bar. To my horror, when we got home that evening, I discovered Jack had an uncontrollable temper just like my dad. He'd gotten irate for seemingly no reason at all, and I freaked out as he set about wrecking the apartment. He was angry a lot after that. It was as if some monster had been unleashed inside him, and it didn't take long for him to turn his wrath on me.

With a new baby in tow, Jack soon found other outlets to vent his fury; he began having affairs. In fact, he had been having affairs all along, but I could barely bring myself to say anything for fear of sending him over the edge and getting the crap beat out of me.

One night, I sat pensively on the sofa in our apartment. I could hear him in the bedroom already stumbling drunk and preparing to go out. I'd fed the boys and put them to bed early while I summoned the nerve to confront him. I wanted him to stop cheating on me. He was my husband, and he needed to start acting like it.

THE UNCHAINED

"I'm going out," he announced, opening the door to leave.

"Would you please just stay home tonight?"

"I've got something I need to take care of."

"Something or someone?"

I knew I'd taken a calculated misstep when the door slammed and I felt the sting of his hand across my face. He snatched me up from the sofa and smacked me again. I fell backward and came down hard on the floor.

"Stop!" Matthew screamed. "Stop hurting my mommy!"

I looked up through blood and tears and saw my beautiful boy standing in the doorway leading up the hall to his room. He just stood crying and begging Jack to leave me alone. I scrambled over to him and grabbed him up. He wrapped his arms around my neck and held on tightly. Jack pulled himself together, spat some expletive and stormed out of the apartment.

Matthew was growing up to be a very intuitive child. Watching me go through the hell I was going through with Jack, I knew he was old enough to understand. Even at his age, I'm sure he had issues of his own, never really getting the chance to know his biological father. My diet consisted of healthy doses of remorse and recrimination because I denied both of them the privilege. At 8 years old, I could see how disappointed he was as he sat with his suitcase, waiting for the plane ticket Harold promised to send so he could visit him in Illinois — the ticket that never arrived.

HIDDEN TREASURE

My toxic merry-go-round with Jack went on for four years. He'd move out, and I'd keep letting him back in. Jack was one of those types who when he was good, he was so good to me, but when he was bad, it was horrible. It wasn't so much the physical abuse as it was the other women that was more traumatic for me.

At one point, he even sold all the furniture in the house with the exception of the kids' stuff just so he could have money to buy a pound of marijuana. His rationale was he would sell it and make more money to buy better furniture.

"What are you doing this for? This is crazy." I was falling apart. "Jack, I can't do this anymore. I just can't."

He scoffed and went into another room to make a call. I could hear him on the phone telling someone, "I can't see you tonight because Doreen's having a breakdown."

My "breakdown" landed me in the psych ward of St. Vincent's Hospital for a week. I got up one morning and called home, and a neighbor answered the phone. Jack had left the kids and had been with his girlfriend the entire time.

Still trying to hold onto the dilapidated remains of what there was between us, I got pregnant again. Because Jack wasn't working, I found myself pulling 50-hour weeks just to keep a roof over our heads. I came home one night exhausted, reeking of spaghetti sauce from the Italian restaurant where I worked and found him and the boys lounging in front of the television.

"Jack, this place is filthy. You know my aunt is coming

in today."

"What do you want me to do about it?"

"I want you to do more than lay around and watch TV all day. Do you really expect me to do everything?"

The silence that followed was so loud it had a sound like the approach of rolling thunder. Two months pregnant and overworked, my hormones had me on edge. I wasn't sure whether my outburst would ignite his fuse, but at that point, I was too tired to care.

"Okay, I'll clean up."

I was taken aback by his response.

"You go and get a shower. I'll take care of the housework."

I went in and got cleaned up, and Jack did what he said he was going to do. The respite was short-lived. My aunt arrived, and we put her in the spare room. That night, Jack started hitting me, and despite my futile attempt to be quiet, my aunt heard from the adjoining bathroom.

"Doreen, are you all right in there?"

"Yes," I whimpered, trying to muffle my tears. "I'm fine."

But I wasn't, and she knew it. She was mortified by Jack's behavior and asked that I take her to a hotel the next morning. She told me she would not be coming back and encouraged me to leave, as well. I didn't. I couldn't. But I did make a decision right then that I couldn't have another child, so I scheduled an abortion.

The room was sterile and antiseptic. Fluorescent lights buzzed overhead. I shook as I lay on the table, staring at the ceiling, waiting for the procedure to begin. The nurse systematically checked my vitals, and I watched dully as if viewing from afar. This wasn't me — it was someone else. But it was me, and I was afraid. In my heart, I knew what was happening was the right thing; there was no other choice. Even if I wanted to keep the baby, I still might lose it because of the beatings. That would be more than I could bear.

"Are you ready, Doreen?" the doctor asked.

"Yes, but I want you to do something else for me."

"What?"

"I want you to tie my tubes."

"Are you sure?"

"Yes." I desperately grabbed the doctor's arm. "But you can't tell Jack. Promise me."

She nodded. An eternity later, it was over.

Open Doors

Two months after my medical procedure, we found ourselves in counseling. The fact that I had my tubes tied gradually came out in our sessions. Jack exploded.

"You did what?"

"How was I supposed to have another baby when we barely make ends meet now?"

"You could have told me, Doreen."

"It was my decision. I'm the only one with a job!"

The revelation that I was not going to have another child with him must have been just what he needed to set

THE UNCHAINED

Jack on another course, and he got a job. A year later, things had gotten a little better — at least financially. I was working another job, making more money, and we no longer needed public assistance. But by then, the government found out what we were doing, and we were both charged with welfare fraud, which is a felony. Surprisingly, Jack attempted to take full responsibility, but that wasn't the way it was going to go. We were both put on probation and ordered to pay restitution.

Our neighbor, Cathy, was a bright spot during those trying days. She'd saved me from Jack's violent temper on more than one occasion by calling the police, and over time, she and I became friends. Cathy was a Christian, and I'd been honest with her about what was going on between Jack and me. Several times, she prayed with me, and we talked about the love of Jesus and what a difference he could make in my life if I let him. Her enthusiasm and compassion stirred inside me and made me hunger for more. She told me stories about people she'd known and how God had changed them. I thought it was wonderful, but that type of thing could never happen for me.

Cathy's energy was exciting, and I remember thinking I wanted to be just like her, to have this thing she had that gave her so much joy. I needed to be anointed with this incredible entity she referred to as the Holy Spirit. She invited some friends to her apartment, and we prayed, and one of the women told me I had the "gift of healing." I had no idea what that meant. It scared me to think I would start praying in some language I didn't understand. Still, it was cool, this gift she spoke about. I laughed when I thought that maybe it meant I was supposed to go out and be a paramedic or something.

I started going to Cathy's church in Beaverton, Oregon — not far from my present church, Evergreen Christian Center — and unexpectedly, Jack did, as well. Whether overwhelmed by emotion or a desire for God, I invited him into my heart — I just didn't allow him to really be a part of my life. The lure of alcohol and the need to anesthetize my pain was still too strong. I wasn't ready. It wasn't time for me then. But the door had been opened, and it was enough to keep me going back from time to time.

One of the conditions of Jack's probation was that he couldn't drink. By this time, I'd become pretty friendly with the probation officer, and he told me if Jack were to give me any trouble or start hitting me, I could give him a call, and he'd have him arrested. The strength I'd gained from the church and being fed up with being his punching bag drove me to make the call. Jack had been drinking and was preparing to step out on me again, and I was finally over it. Because of his violation, the judge decided he no longer wanted to deal with him and kept him locked up. At long last, he was out of my life, but I needed him out of my system, so I started partying again.

Two months passed before Jack was released from jail. He was down on his luck and had no place to go. Being a chronic enabler, I let him stay with me. He wanted to borrow my truck to go out, and he dropped me off at my favorite watering hole while the kids were at home with the babysitter. Not having a ride home, the bouncer asked one of the guys he knew to give me a lift. "Don't worry. He's okay," he told me. So, I trusted him. I was grateful not to have to walk.

"Thanks for bringing me home."

"Not a problem."

He pulled up to my complex, turned off the key in the ignition and got out with me.

"You know, this really isn't necessary. I can make it from here."

"I don't mind walking you up."

When we reached my apartment, I turned to him to say thank you as I opened the door. He leered at me and pushed his way in.

Why didn't I stop him? Why didn't I scream or do something? Why did I just let it happen? I was afraid for myself. I was afraid for my boys. The man took an almost sadistic pleasure in violating me with my children in the other room. He hurt me — physically. I stuck my arm in my mouth and bit down to keep from screaming. It was horrible. I just wanted it to be over.

Again, I didn't report it. This was the second time I allowed myself to be victimized. My self-esteem was crushed. I told myself, *If you live this kind of lifestyle, this sort of thing is going to keep happening. You must deserve it. It wouldn't be happening otherwise.* True or not, that's how I felt. There were so many men. So much hurt. I had to find a way out.

HIDDEN TREASURE

An Uncommon Man

I was 29 years old when I met Larry. I was pretty drunk, playing pinball in a bar, and he came up to me drinking a Coke. As I recall, he had an easy laugh and a pleasant smile, but he remembers more about the night than I do considering I was nearly blacked out. I suppose even in my inebriated state it had to be one heck of an introduction because he called the next day.

"What time's dinner?"

"Who are you?"

"It's Larry ... from last night."

Apparently, I'd asked him over. My mind was like mush trying to figure out to whom I was talking.

"Um, 6 p.m., I guess."

Anxious and a little uneasy as the time drew closer, I still had no clue. This guy could have been a stalker or Jack the Ripper for all I knew. He was late, and I'd had several glasses of wine by the time he arrived. The boys and I were looking out the window when he drove up.

"I guess this guy's name is Larry. He's coming to dinner, boys. He's got a car and a job. This is great!"

He said he had a flat tire on the way, which caused the delay. The boys had already eaten, and I'd put his plate aside. We laughed and talked, and I discovered he was four years older than me; he'd also never been married before and had no children. My interest was piqued. Jack the Ripper he was not. The boys seemed to like him a lot. They played together and wrestled around in the floor just the way I imagined a father should do with his sons. Larry stayed that night, and it appeared that he was in no hurry to leave. He joked that he'd hang around at least four years — with options. It appeared that the third time was the charm.

The first two weeks, though, I stayed drunk because he was way too nice, and I wasn't used to being treated that way. On our first official date, he took me to the movies. I didn't understand why we were there. I hadn't gone to a theater in years because there was no drinking at the movies.

Larry was an unusual and genuine man. He and I started attending church regularly with the kids. Things were finally turning around. About three and a half years into these uncharted waters, I felt sure God was saying it's time.

"Your four-year option is up," I told him. "Either we get married, or you can leave."

For the first time in my life, I wore a white wedding gown and veil. The boys were ushers in their adorable grey tuxedos with pink cummerbunds; they were so excited. Among the 100 or so guests were relatives from out of state, and even Jack's parents showed up. I gave his mother a small bouquet of flowers to let her know how much I loved her, no matter what happened between her son and me. All in all, it was a beautiful day.

I'd been attending church and going through the motions for nearly 10 years, but I never formed a true relationship with Christ. I was compulsively involved with the youth soccer team, coaching and administrating seven days a week, so much so that I eventually stopped going to church altogether. I prayed and read the Bible a little, but I was just "too busy" for church.

I was diagnosed with Multiple Sclerosis shortly after Larry and I were married. In October of 2003, tortured by the pain of arthritis, alternating between a cane and a walker, I was nearly crippled by despair. We had very little money, and frustration over whether or not we'd be able to pay the next month's rent pushed us to the brink of desperation. There were even times when I did without medication just to keep the heat on.

"God, help us," I cried.

Sometimes you don't realize God is what you need, until God is all you have. I told Larry it was imperative that we return to church. There was a reason all this was happening, and that was the only place I knew to turn.

We decided to attend Evergreen Christian. The moment we entered, I felt at home. I knew the Lord was calling out to me, and he had never left me. I was going to be okay from that day on.

The first of manifested miracles occurred eight years later. Living on social security and not being able to work, every waking moment seemed a constant battle. Prayer was my only consolation.

"God, you have me here for a reason. You've seen me through every pitfall in my life. Please heal me — let me live."

The beauty and simplicity of God's grace is a miracle

in itself. I was cured through prayer, and I finally began to see my gift was designed so I could be a living testament to the healing virtue of God. In 2006, I had a double knee replacement, which was followed by a shoulder replacement in 2007. Baffling the doctors, I healed twice as fast as expected; they, too, had to realize there was a greater power at work.

With God's help and the love of a good man, I was finally able to stop drinking. Clean and sober for 23 years, the Lord has revealed himself in a whole new light. Larry and I have been attending Evergreen Christian Center for a while now. And within the last year, this treasure that has been buried inside me opened up in the most amazing way. What it means to have the gift of healing becomes clearer every day as I submit my life to the Lord Jesus and become a new Doreen. Salvation is a wonderful thing. All of this time, it's been the missing piece of the puzzle.

As I have learned the power of God's mercy, I have had to learn how to forgive myself and the people around me and let go of my past mistakes and failures. The Lord is showing me daily how to be kind, loving and understanding. Every time I turn around, there's somebody else with whom I am able to share God's goodness and faithfulness. I share what I've gone through in my life to let other women know no one has the right to look down on you because of your past. The Lord has healed me from all these things and forgiven me, and I know he can forgive them, too.

Because of what I've experienced, I can say to people I

did go through those things, but the person I was then is not who I am now. The only thing that brought me to this point was the grace and love of God, even though, most of the time, I wasn't aware he was here. I thought I was in control — time and again, it was proven that I wasn't. I've been reminded of the promise the Lord made to me when I was 14 years old, crying out for help: "Doreen, I will always take care of you." And he's done just that!

AGAINST ALL HUMAN ODDS
The Story of Evan Acey
Written by Christee Wise

Burning with fever, I lay there listening to the rain drumming on the tent. The pounding in my head amplified the excruciating beat. My 14-year-old body ached like it was 100. Racked by a coughing fit, I doubled up and pressed my head against the dilapidated pillow to try and stop the throbbing. Painfully, I drew the worn sleeping bag around me and gathered it under my chin as I suddenly broke out in chills.

The dank bag offered little warmth or padding. It and a thin layer of canvas tarp was all that separated me from the cold, hard ground. A former Boy Scout, I'd expertly dug a trench around the tent to keep the rain from trickling into the humble shelter. But the trench had become a moat, and if the rain continued at its present rate, my domicile would be wholly flooded, its ragged protection gone.

I'd been homeless for nearly seven months. The mild Oregon weather had been tolerable, until it began to rain and didn't stop. On school days, I had some place to go and even to shower, but an incident with Principal Thompson ended that.

"Acey, you're late." Adults had such a knack for stating the obvious.

"No kidding?"

His arm shot out, and his hand grabbed the larger portion of my unkempt hair, which he was using as a handle to drag me in the direction of his office.

By reflex, I threw a block with one arm, spun and shoved my shoulder into his chest, driving him backward and pinning him against a wall full of lockers.

"That's it!" he erupted, pushing me off. "You're out!" I had already started for the door. "And don't come back!"

No one would be following up on me for truancy.

Actually, I could probably die and rot out here on Elk Island, and no one would know. They'd find my remains 10 years from now and have to bring in a special team to use my dental records or DNA to figure out who I was. Ralph isn't going to be looking for me as a missing person. He's the one who kicked me out of the house. Mom would probably feel pretty badly, but Ralph, he'd be happy I was dead. Maybe sorry he didn't get to kill me. God knows he's come close.

My mother and stepfather moved from North Portland to a farm out in the country while I was gone. Eventually, the severity of the flu took a toll even on my pride, and I concluded I had no choice but to find their place and see if they'd let me move back in with them.

My absence and return made no substantial difference in terms of Ralph. He continued to attack me physically whenever he was angry, which was most of the time. Daily, since I was 4 years old, almost as if it was an essential component of my upbringing like teaching me to brush my teeth, he reminded me, "You're worthless! You'll never amount to anything."

AGAINST ALL HUMAN ODDS

Rarely did a day go by that I wasn't bloodied or bruised by an enraged assault from my stepfather. When I was younger, I tried to figure out what fired his hair-triggered wrath but soon learned there was no telling what could set him off. One moment, he'd be smiling and the next, *Wham!* He'd given me a free flight to the next county.

Mother's marriage to Ralph pooled four children each and made a household of 10. Ralph had four daughters older than me. I already had two older sisters and a younger sister. None of the girls ever seemed to stir the violent attention that I, the only son, inspired.

Gilligan had just botched another of the survivors' attempts to get off the island, and the Skipper was ready to let Gilligan have it with his hat. It was hot and the front door stood open to let some breeze move through the house as I sat on the floor watching my favorite show. I was 7.

Suddenly, the floor was no longer beneath me. Suspended by my hair, I dangled from my stepfather's firm grip. Unleashing a stream of profanity, he kicked and punched me in the back and legs several times as he crossed the room.

"What in the hell were you thinking?" he managed to pronounce amid the ranting and screaming and cursing. Turning, he grasped me with both hands and flung me back across the room. I sprawled across the solid frame of the couch and drizzled down the face of it into a mass of shocked and shattered flesh. My brain and body were battling to take hold on separate fronts and couldn't cope with what was happening or communicate with each other.

Ralph left me laying there and stomped from the room.

Ralph had a car on which he was working on up on jacks in the driveway. Discovering it had fallen or been pushed from the jacks, he came straight after me. I was the scapegoat for that one. Even after the truth came to light, that one of my stepsister's boyfriends had knocked it down, I never received an apology or any recognition whatsoever of my innocence.

Ralph's fury seemed to spill over onto me. When his rage was released, there was nothing to stay its power. I was like a receptacle, and by the time I was 8, I was filled with so much anger, it began to spill out of me.

I stood in front of the hobby shop staring into the window. During business hours a model train traveled around the store on elevated tracks, passing the window every few minutes. Hanging from the ceiling were several radio-controlled airplanes that were, in my eyes, almost as big as the real thing. There was every type of miniature anything that you could imagine in that store, from trains, planes and cars, to doll houses and furniture, farm animals, plastic horses to collect and the supplies to do every kind of project known to father and son. My heart broke at the thought. There were no father-son moments for me. Why should some people have so much happiness and then some of us have nothing but pain?

AGAINST ALL HUMAN ODDS

Without thinking, I picked up a broken brick and flung it with all my 8-year-old might through the plate glass. I grabbed everything I could get in my hands and carry and headed straight for the alley. Several blocks later, I sat down to catch my breath and to look at the spoils I'd plundered from Harvey's House of Hobbies. Then it dawned on me how much trouble I would be in when Ralph discovered I was a thief. I didn't even get to enjoy the things I'd stolen. It was a waste of time.

Most of my third-grade year, though, was spent in Minneapolis. Up to then, Mother had been a regular recipient of Ralph's abuse, as well.

"I'm done," she told him. "I swear you've hit me for the last time. I'm leaving."

She packed up her four children, including me, and drove to Minnesota. After almost a year, we came back. Ralph wised up where she was concerned. But I guess he figured there was no real problem if he took it out on me instead. He still thought of me as his personal punching bag.

I acted out in anger, and nearly always, this brought further recrimination.

"You know what's going to happen when Ralph gets home!" my mother shouted. She thrust a dusty Bible open to the Ten Commandments at me and told me to start memorizing.

I'd been caught stealing from a G.I. Joe's store.

Ashamed, defeated and terrified, I took the book and headed to my room where I sat trembling and trying to develop a working knowledge of the Holy Bible to save my life. "Thou shalt not ..." I repeated over and over, straining to listen for my stepfather over the thunder of my heart and the roar in my ears.

At the sound of his footfall on the stairs, I broke into a sweat and chanted the words frantically, rapidly, miserably anticipating a beating like none I'd ever had.

The irate man crashed through the door and towered over me. I pushed myself back as far as I could into one corner of my room. Drawing my knees up, I held the book open against them. The stiff black cover had grown damp where I clutched it on the side edges.

I stopped breathing.

"Whadya' learn, boy?" he roared.

"Th ... thou ... ssshaalt ... not ... steal?" I squeaked it out as a question, using the four words and punctuation to plead my case.

He seemed not to hear. "If you're gonna steal," he threatened, "you'd better learn to do it like me and not get caught."

I stared in disbelief as he turned and walked out of the room.

Limp with amazement and relief, I melted face first to the floor.

***

"Hey, li'l bro', you wanna drag?"

I looked at the joint my sister held.

AGAINST ALL HUMAN ODDS

"Take it, man," one of their boyfriends said laughing. "You can tell your friends you got stoned. They'll think you're the coolest." They burst into gales of laughter.

My parents didn't condone drugs in the house. But when they weren't around, there were plenty passed around. With six older sisters, there were also teenaged guys. It was a game to get me high. I was smoking and doing drugs long before I became a teenager.

Although my stepfather focused his physical violence on me, no one in the family escaped without emotional scars. Drug use, self-injury, severe depression and unexplainable illness of all kinds are just a few examples of the results — bitterness exacting judgment from the inside out.

Wherever his fury originated, it seemed to come out mostly on me. Without an outlet, I contained the anger within myself where it smoldered and sparked and grew white-hot. I was just a few degrees short of a practiced felon and would arrive there, no doubt, by the time I was a teenager.

Leslie, my best friend, was in love again. He had a crush on the new girl in his class, and there was nothing he wouldn't do to be with her. She invited him to her church, North Baptist. Of course, Les didn't want to go by himself, and so he asked me to come along, and I agreed, having no idea what it meant.

Whatever I expected, I was completely surprised. The people were warm and genuinely cared about me. Starved for this kind of love, I decided I wanted to go back again.

THE UNCHAINED

It actually reminded me of the stories of the Bible my mother read to me when I needed comfort. In fact, I became a regular in the 10-year-old Sunday school class.

One Sunday, I woke up after taking an awful beating from Ralph the night before. I carried some attitude with me when I headed into church. After an hour of watching and listening to all the people bubbling over with joy and love for each other, the dry tinder of frustration in my heart ignited and burst into flames.

I slammed into the men's bathroom and began karate kicking at the doors and walls. "You people have no right to be so d*** happy!" I sobbed in complete surrender to the contempt I felt.

Thrusting my fist through a window, I didn't care about pain or blood. "You stupid people have no idea what it's like out there in the real world!" I shouted. "Well, I'll show you what it's like out there. This," I tore the soap dispenser from the wall and smashed it against the floor, "is what it's like in the real world!"

The door opened and in walked my Sunday school teacher. I saw the displeasure flash in his eyes and immediately sunk to the floor by the sink, ready for the beating I deserved. I fully expected him to attack me, drag me out by the collar and throw me into the street. But in his nice suit and tie, he knelt down on the floor and then turned to sit with his back against the wall next to me.

"Evan, I know you're having trouble at home." He reached out very gently to put his hand on my shoulder. "I'd like to pray for you. Would that be okay?"

I was speechless, not with fear, but with disbelief. I'd destroyed these people's property, and he was sitting on the floor wanting to pray for me. I sobbed into my arms folded on my upraised knees. The dam was opened; pain and anger came spilling and rushing out in agonizing gasps.

He began to pray, "Lord, you know Evan is having a really hard time right now. I want to ask you to work a miracle in his heart. Help him learn to trust you and let you love him. Amen."

"Son, I'm thinking that you're going to need to work around the church to pay for the damage. But I think if we can work that out, there's no need to tell your folks about what's happened here." He held out a hand to shake on it, man to man.

Had that genuine Christ-follower not been there, had he reacted in anger or in punishment, I would have taken this in with the rest of my resentment, and it would have stayed there. But he gave me an opportunity to pour out the ugliness and to allow my heart to receive some of God's infinite love and grace.

I have to know what makes these people so different, I thought.

Each Saturday night for the next year, I ironed my own shirt so on Sunday morning, I could get up and head to Sunday school. My perfect attendance in Sunday school earned me a little recognition, and at the end, I was given my own Bible as a reward. Nothing has meant more to anyone than that Bible has meant to me.

THE UNCHAINED

Under the covers, flashlight in hand, I read to learn more about the man named Jesus who they talked about at church. Jesus' power, love and kindness overwhelmed me, and I felt something like a deep friendship forming in my heart with him.

I had come to the part in the New Testament where soldiers came and took Jesus while he was praying in a garden. They arrested him, took him back and without being able to prove any charges, beat him until he was bloody and bruised. They spit in his face. Jesus! The one who'd healed their sick and blind and lame, had brought joy into their hearts.

Overcome with indignation, I threw the Bible to the floor and sobbed into my pillow. *How could they treat the innocent one this way? Didn't they know he was the son of God? He never did anything to you,* I wailed mentally at the soldiers and people.

Instantly, I identified with Christ. I knew how he felt, and it dawned on me that he knew how I felt. Innocent and beaten, we were intimately connected. I knew I was not completely innocent, but he was. And I knew the significance of his grace. I'd seen it in my Sunday school teacher.

Finally, I picked up the book again and read on. I was amazed to discover Jesus didn't strike all his enemies with lightening. He laid his life down, as they nailed him to the cross and left him to die. I was astounded with what Jesus prayed, "Father, forgive them, for they know not what they do."

From that point, I was changed. My circumstances didn't change, nor did I become a saint. But the presence of God changed me and changed the course of my life. The circumstances from which I came statistically aligned me to end up a crime-committing, wife-beating child abuser. But that is not what God had planned for me.

A couple years after I came to know Christ, or he introduced himself to me, we moved, and I was no longer able to attend North Baptist Church. Not having any family connections to church, I didn't know how to seek out a church. My faith was still very real, I knew and loved Christ, but I had no real support. The "good, solid Christian" kids probably never realized I was one of them.

"Hey, new kid!" someone called from the back of the bus my first day at the new school in Tigard. Everyone piled his or her school supplies on the seat next to him or her or scooted to the middle of the bus, to demonstrate there was no room for me.

The group that accepted me was made up of the kids who sat at the back of the bus — the hoods, the potheads, the stoners. This is where I felt accepted. I wasn't totally at ease there, either, but it was better than being alone.

My friends have often mentioned they knew I was different. They thought sometimes it was funny to watch my discomfort as they pressured me to take another toke on the passing marijuana joint, or when they schemed to cause trouble, break into stores or homes and steal. Since the day I met Jesus, when the anger was taken from my heart and he said he'd be with me all the time, I had not wanted to fight or hurt people, or to tear up property or steal. I did drugs to fit in with a group, but my heart wasn't dark anymore.

***

It was late, and I knew I'd be dead if anyone heard me coming in at that time. Slipping off my shoes, I headed up the stairs, avoiding the third one because it squeaked terribly.

"What's this?" Ralph demanded, holding up a small plastic bag filled with dried and crushed green leaves the next morning. He knew it was pot. I shrugged.

He grabbed me by the front of the shirt and jammed me up against the wall, growling into my face. "I said, 'What is this?'"

"Pot." I knew I was a goner. It must have fallen out of my pocket the night before.

"Well, you little S.O.B.," he sneered, "you think you can do what you want under my roof? Who gave you permission to bring drugs into this house?"

"Nobody."

"Well, get the hell out! Get out of my house!" He gave me a hard shove and then flung me toward the door.

I never came back to that house. I was homeless until sickness drove me to find them again.

Of course, when I returned, the violence started right up again. But in a couple years, I had grown a little stronger. I was 15 or 16, and Ralph lost his temper and came after me. He flew at me with his fist ready. A look of surprise and maybe a little fear crossed his face when I knocked his hand away and threw him off balance. Seizing the advantage, I wrestled him to the ground. He fought to the point of exhaustion and finally conceded, "Okay, you're big enough and strong enough to kick my butt. You can do whatever you want, but you'd better find yourself somewhere else to live, because you are no longer welcome here."

I'd given up on high school after being kicked out of yet another one for showing up drunk. As soon as I finished my GED, I enrolled in college and at 17, moved out on my own. Sometimes I worked as many as three jobs, but I put myself through school and earned my degree.

Although I wasn't yet free from a distractive life problem, I did believe in Jesus Christ, and when I used faith, he never let me down. I'm sure there are those who could never see past the drug use and other behaviors to trust that I truly was a Christian. Some may have doubted he made a difference simply because I was not attending church and actively witnessing. But the difference God made in my life was in terms of where I might have been without him. He had started a work in me. It was later that my eyes were opened to my need to not compromise walking with Christ by whatever I wanted and abusing his grace. The odds, humanly speaking, were not in my favor. But Christ was.

The Lord Jesus Christ was and is now even more an absolute constant in my life. His presence saved my life.

THE UNCHAINED

No one is perfect except for him, and his perfection is what covers our imperfections, shortcomings and sins. He put within me a deep desire to live a moral life and know him. From the first time he intervened in the men's bathroom at North Baptist Church in Portland, Oregon, he never left me. Several times, I have had encounters with him in which I felt he was speaking to me directly. Since I was not a regular church attendee, I suppose he spoke to me in a way I would hear, very clearly and very directly.

Occasionally, he sent people into my life to speak the truth I needed to hear. Because I could tell they had a real relationship with Jesus, I was able to hear.

One such person was Keith. I worked for Keith in his roofing business while I was going to college. He was far from ignorant about the drug abuse of his crew, but he was non-confrontational.

We sat in his truck one day, eating lunch and talking.

"I need to get hold of my brother-in-law," I commented. "My car won't pass the DEQ inspection for licensing in city limits. If he'll let me register my car to his address out in the country, it won't have to pass DEQ."

We were quiet for a few seconds, finishing our sandwiches.

Keith pulled a piece of straw out of the funny old hat he wore all the time and began to pick his teeth with it.

"Y'know, Evan. I thought about using my brother's address out there to do the same thing. Then it occurred to me — would Jesus borrow an address to register his car to get around the law?" He went on picking his teeth and letting me think about the question. I knew he was right. Jesus wouldn't do it, and neither could I.

I was 19 when God began a process of calling me back to him.

By this time, I was abusing drugs heavily. I smoked pot regularly, used several other drugs and had started using meth. Again, the true desire in my heart to be responsible and moral was still there. I had a $10-a-day pot habit to support. I had to get money from somewhere. Many of my friends resorted to stealing to support their drug habits, but not me. I could never do it. Jesus wouldn't let me.

Sitting on the front steps of my house, I took a long drag on a cigarette and exhaled slowly. It was habitual, but it was relaxing, just sitting there smoking, thinking and watching the world go by. Summer, my 2 year old, played in the yard and toddled up to offer me leaves, rocks and various other treasures she discovered.

"Hi," a passerby waved up at me from the sidewalk. He was a friendly man, maybe mids-20s, close to my age. After some neighborly small talk, he explained, "We're starting a new church out here in Oregon City, and I'd just like to let you know you're welcome to come and check it out."

My wife, who wasn't a Christian at the time, and I were not actively looking for a church, but there was an affirmation in my heart that here was a man who was one of the genuine Christians who knew Christ in a real way. The whole exchange, which lasted less than five minutes, was a reminder from the Lord.

A couple of weeks went by, and again, I went out for a

smoke. Millions of stars dotted the sky, and I began to consider God. As soon as my mind turned to him, I felt his presence there. It was as though an old friend walked right up the steps, stood directly in front of me, looked into my eyes and said, "I want you to take your children to church. I am going to pour out my spirit on your family and secure their future."

I approached my wife. "You know, we need to go to church. I think God's wanting me to get back into a church and for us to take the kids."

Her reaction was less than enthusiastic, "That's all I need."

But I called some old friends who I knew were real Christians and asked where they were going to church. The next Sunday, we went to church with Eric and Kathy. It was like coming home. I made a decision to be closer to the Lord from that day forward. And from then on, I never smoked another joint, took another drug or scored another hit of anything. It was not because of my determination or willpower, either. God simply removed the addiction and the desire.

A few weeks later, I was baptized.

We became active in that church, and our children were involved in activities.

Sitting in my former party room turned prayer room a month or so after I was baptized, I was smoking.

"Evan, I've healed you," I heard God say.

Cool, I thought, thinking he was talking about the drugs.

But he went on, "Evan, I've healed you. And I have even cleansed your body. If you continue to pollute it by smoking cigarettes, you *will* get cancer."

Immediately, I removed the unfinished cigarette and crushed it dead in the ashtray. I have not smoked since. Jesus removed this habit for me.

Jesus continues to be as real to me today as he was when I was 10, 12, 17, 19 and 23. He continues to change me.

***

Kevin was a wheelchair-bound acquaintance for whom I'd done some work prior to these events. By chance, I saw him wheeling down the sidewalk near my house one night. It was nearly midnight. I hurried out to talk with him, anxious to let him know what Jesus had done and could do.

"What are you up to?" I asked him.

"Well, I kind of got turned around and lost. I haven't been in this area for a while. I'm looking for the bus," he said.

"It's about five blocks up," I said. "I'll walk you."

As we walked, I told him I'd met Jesus, and I wasn't using pot or meth anymore. "Kevin, God's worked a miracle in my life."

I watched as Kevin got onto the bus, and then I turned around and headed home, walking and talking some more with my friend, Jesus.

THE UNCHAINED

Nine years went by. I was downtown making a delivery, and I heard someone yell, "Evan!"

Turning on the sidewalk, I saw Kevin pushing the big wheels of his chair to catch me. He had a wide smile on his face. "Hey, Kevin! It's been a really long time."

Reaching out his hand to shake mine, he excitedly jumped in to tell me the story of the night we'd met eight or nine years before. "Evan, you stopped me on Foster Road that night about midnight. You told me about Jesus. I wasn't lost; I knew where I was. I was going up to 82nd Street to catch a bus. My life was so horrible, I was going to take a bus to downtown Portland, find a boat dock and wheel myself off and take my life."

He continued looking me squarely in the eyes. "But I knew what you were like at the time you worked for me. And I knew that what you had that night when I saw you was real. And I wanted to find out about it, too. So, I found myself a church."

"Evan, I am alive today because you stopped me and told me Jesus touched you. I'm a deacon in my church." Tears had formed in his eyes, as they were now doing in mine.

Jesus is real. I saw it in my Sunday school teacher, in Eric and Keith; now Kevin had seen it in me. I was changed. Now Kevin was changed. What changes will those who meet Kevin see and experience?

Others in my immediate family, including my mother, witnessed the changes in my life and were drawn to Christ. As it turns out, my mother experienced a faith in

Christ when she was younger, but then life had taken her down a different path. She also found herself returning to her "first love" and the fellowship of a good church.

Ralph divorced her after all the children were gone. I drove out to the farm a couple of years after I was "recalled" to talk with him. It was important for me to tell him that I forgave him. God directed me to do this, much like Jesus' posture toward his abusers. I explained to my stepfather I harbored no bitterness, that Jesus had changed the course of my life. Ralph cried and thanked me. Although he made no move toward Jesus that day, I feel like he, too, was exposed to the reality of Christ. I know that, in spite of the odds, God can and does make a difference.

The promise that God gave — that he would pour out his spirit and secure the future of my children — is being fulfilled. Tragically, my first marriage did not survive. The Lord never left me. He was as real in the darkest of days as he is in the most joyful times. That again is the reality of Christ that inspires my faith and encourages others as well.

I met Tamera in the spring.

We'd been dating for a while, and she'd heard me speak frequently about my friend Jesus and how I talked to and learned from the Lord. Raised as a Jehovah's Witness, she did not understand my relationship with Christ. She left that group several years earlier and had no relationship with God at all.

We were riding in her car one night when she said, "I have to have my dad look at my brakes."

THE UNCHAINED

"Why?" I asked.

"Because they're squeaking."

"Really, I don't hear them."

"Oh, that's funny," she replied. "You can hear God, but you can't hear my brakes!"

Tamera and I have now been married eight years.

"I can tell you have a belief that is very real to you, Evan," Tamera would say every once in a while. "You have something I don't really understand. And you genuinely believe God takes care of you."

A year and a half ago, Tamera also had an encounter. She has come to know for herself the God that accepts us where we are and changes us from the inside out. Together, we have been attending Evergreen Christian Center.

Those around me can witness the plan God has for me — to not return evil for evil, but instead return good toward evil and help lift those burdened down like I was before I came to know him.

God reached down and intervened so I would not have to carry the anger, bitterness and violence with me. Because he has always been there, he led me through the most difficult of times. At regular intervals in my life, he gently reminded me of his presence and the desire he had to change me. Against all human odds, God set me free from hate, bitterness, anger and addiction. His friendship is genuine. His salvation is real. His grace is fathomless. His love has no limits.

MESSAGES FROM THE SKY
The Story of Cindy
Written by Peggy Thompson

He ducked behind the shrubbery along the side of the building and watched for signs of activity. It was early morning, and most people were getting up, preparing to start their day. Flicking his cigarette out onto the lawn, he decided to make his move. Cautiously, he moved out of the shrubbery and slowly made his way to the stairway of the apartment building. Pausing on the landing, he glanced around quickly in all directions, then quietly mounted the stairs. When he reached #12, he paused. His gut contracted with anticipation. He loved these adventures. Placing his hand on the doorknob, he slowly turned it, holding his breath, hoping it wouldn't make a sound. To his surprise, the door opened. It was unlocked.

Entering the tiny living room, he gently pushed the door shut until he heard a little click. As he stood there, perspiration dotting his forehead and upper lip, he heard sounds coming from the bedroom. He crept a little closer in the direction of the sounds and then stopped. She was humming softly, and he expelled a little sigh of relief. She hadn't heard him. Quickly, he tiptoed to the kitchen where he saw a knife laying on the sink. He grabbed it and headed back to where he could watch her.

He flattened himself against the wall by the doorway and edged close enough to peek through the narrow opening created by the open door. The light was on in the bedroom. She was getting dressed, and his excitement increased. She opened a drawer in the dresser and pulled out a pair of nylons.

Throwing himself into the room, he roared, "Caroline!"

She whirled to face him, terror written on her face, her eyes huge like a doe caught in the headlights of a car.

He reached her in a few giant strides as he brandished the knife. She opened her mouth to scream, but he was too fast for her. He smashed her in the mouth with the heel of his hand. With his other hand, he gave her a severe wrench that twisted her around so he was in back of her. His arm wrapped around her, locking her arms tightly to her sides. He plunged the knife into the soft flesh of her belly and shivered with the thrill of it. "Can't ignore me now, can you?" He stabbed her several more times, then grabbed a nylon stocking from the bed. Wrapping it around her neck, he pulled it taut.

She was bleeding profusely and making a gagging sound. Suddenly, her legs went limp beneath her, and as she sagged to the floor, he dragged her by the knotted nylon into the bathroom where he tied the other end to the faucet in the bathtub. Her lifeless form lay there awkwardly. "Got what you deserved," he panted in a husky voice. He stared at the body for a few more seconds. Adrenalin was racing through his veins. He was excited. Knowing he had to get out of there, he quickly made his way to the front door, looked out and, seeing no one, ran down the stairs and around the side of the building to the alley in the back where he parked his car. He sped away.

***

One morning, when my brother and I woke up, my father told us we were going to go live with my aunt and uncle. My life was about to drastically change — at the age of 4.

Tears began to sting the backs of my eyes. I rubbed at them. "But I don't want to live there. I want to stay here with you and Mama."

My brother, Bill, who was a year older than me, didn't say a word. He just stood there staring as my father pulled two suitcases down from the top of our closet.

"Mama isn't here anymore. After we get your suitcases packed, we'll all go out to breakfast. You'll like that. It'll be fun."

Mama isn't here anymore? I was terrified.

We heard my baby brother, David, crying from the other room, and my father went out and got him.

After breakfast, my father took the three of us to the home of my aunt and uncle. As soon as we got inside the house, he put the suitcases down, returned to the car for David and brought him inside. He put the baby into my aunt's arms, then leaned down and kissed me on the cheek. "Goodbye, Cindy. I'll be back to see you as often as I can." I don't know if he kissed Bill because by then, I had started to cry.

"Don't leave us, Daddy!" I sobbed.

THE UNCHAINED

He left us standing there, and I remember feeling completely abandoned by my father and my mother. It happened overnight. I was in shock.

My aunt handed off the baby to my uncle. She took me by the hand, led me to the couch and pulled me onto her lap.

"There, there, Cindy, honey. Please don't cry." She was cuddling me and stroking my hair with her hand. "We'll take care of you and your brothers. It's going to be all right."

In between sobs, I managed to utter a few words. "Wh… where's my mama? Why did my daddy leave us here? Don't they love us anymore?"

"Of course they do." With a big sigh, she continued, "Your mama and daddy are getting a divorce, Cindy. That means they aren't going to live together anymore."

It was difficult for me to understand. I had never heard the word "divorce."

"Your daddy can't take care of you and your brothers, honey. He has to work and, well, it's difficult for a man to know how to take care of little children all by himself."

I was beginning to calm down a little. "But my mama will want me. Where is she?"

"Your mama did want you, Cindy, but your daddy told her she had to either take you and both your brothers with her or else leave all of you behind. Honey, she's not able to care for the three of you right now, either. She moved away, and she's going to have to get a job."

My 4-year-old brain was trying to make sense of this,

but as I sat quietly in her lap, what I clearly understood was both my parents abandoned us, and I didn't believe I would ever see them again.

My brothers and I lived with my aunt and uncle for about two and a half years. My father came by occasionally to visit, but he never stayed long. He seemed nervous and fidgety around us.

One afternoon, he came to visit, and he brought a woman with him. "Hi, kids. This is a friend of mine. Her name is Justine. Come shake hands."

She seemed cool toward me, but she offered me her hand. I put both of mine behind my back. My aunt served some lemonade and cookies, but I didn't want any. My eyes were glued to Justine and my father. He had his arm around her the whole time, and I thought he had a special look on his face when he looked at her. He used to look at Mama that way sometimes. When they arrived, he didn't even kiss me. He wasn't saying much to me, either, and they didn't stay long. I was upset, and I was jealous.

About a week later, my father came to the house. He was alone this time and sat down to talk to us.

"Justine and I are going to get married. She's going to be your … uh … stepmother."

There was an awkward silence in the room.

"Guess what? We want you children to come live with us." He was beaming.

Jumping up from my spot on the floor, I ran to him and threw my arms around his neck. All I could think about was being home again with my daddy.

THE UNCHAINED

"When? When are we coming to live with you, Daddy?"

"Soon. In two weeks. Right after our wedding."

When I went to bed that night, I tried to remember my mother. Little scenes from long ago flashed through my mind: my mother ironing, her taking pictures of Bill and me (she posed us together to look like we were dancing), a picture of me all by myself with black patent leather shoes, black stretch tights and a white blouse. *How can I remember all the details of that picture of me but nothing about what my mother looked like?* I also remembered lying in bed and being able to see the light from the other room under the door, the TV being on and hearing my parents talking, although I couldn't make out the words. I could even remember we had hardwood floors and bare walls, but my mother was a total blur. It frustrated me so much, I cried into my pillow for hours.

Living with Justine and my father didn't turn out as I expected. She wasn't a loving person and she was a severe disciplinarian. She spanked us a lot and with anything she could get her hands on. She had been pregnant when she married my father, and after the baby was born, she just got worse.

One night, I was getting ready to go to bed.

"Don't forget to go potty, Cindy. Once you're in bed, I don't want you getting up again."

Although I did go potty, after I went to bed, I really did have to go again.

"Justine, I have to go potty," I called to her.

MESSAGES FROM THE SKY

"I told you that you couldn't get up again! Go to sleep!"

There was no way I could go to sleep until I went to the bathroom. She wouldn't let me do that, and I was terrified I would wet the bed.

Remembering there was a laundry basket full of clothes in my closet, I folded back the covers on my bed and tiptoed quietly across my bedroom floor. I snuck into the closet, shut the door behind me, sat on the clothes in the basket and went potty. After that, I was scared she would find out what I had done, but nothing was ever said. I had to do this many times.

The first and only time I can recall my mother visiting us was when I was 7 and Bill was 8. I was in Brownies, and Bill was a Cub Scout. My mother planned to come up from Los Angeles, where she was living, and visit us. It happened to be on a day when Bill had a Cub Scout meeting.

Justine sat us down on the couch one afternoon after school. "Your mother is coming to visit tomorrow. She'll be here sometime after school, but you won't have much time to visit with her. Only a half hour. Bill has a Cub Scout meeting, and I don't want him to miss it."

It took a few seconds to sink in. *My mother is coming! My mother!* My heart was singing. Racing to my room, I threw myself down on the bed and wrapped my arms around myself with excitement. *What will she look like? Is she going to take me home with her?*

My heart was pounding as I flung my closet door open.

THE UNCHAINED

I worked my way through everything I had to wear, and when I saw my pink party dress, I decided I was going to wear it. I pulled it out of the closet and hung it on the doorknob. I would even ask Justine to fasten a pink ribbon in my hair, and I wanted to wear my patent leather shoes.

My imagination ran wild with thoughts of being with my mother, and I felt sure when she saw me, she would not be able to leave me behind again.

As I daydreamed on my bed, Justine came into my room.

"Why is your party dress hanging on the knob?"

"I'm going to wear it tomorrow when I see my mother."

With her hands on her hips, she gave me a smirk. "That's what you think. You will wear your school clothes, just like any other day. Your mother won't be here until you get home from school, and you will only get to see her for a half hour. Do you have any idea how long a half hour is?" She gave me a stern look and snapped her fingers. "Like that!" She walked out of the room.

Justine picked us up after school the next day, just like she always did. "Your mother is waiting for you at the house." She never said another word, and I sat in the backseat with my hands clasped together, eyes shining with almost unbearable excitement.

When we went into the house, I saw her. Standing there, I just looked and looked at her. I tried to fill myself up with the vision of my mother.

She kneeled on the carpet and opened her arms wide

to receive me, her lips parting with the smile of an angel.

I ran into her arms and threw mine around her neck, holding on for dear life. It seemed our two hearts were beating as one as she held me tightly to her breast.

"Cindy. My darling girl." I felt her tears on my cheek.

We stood up together and she looked at me through her teary eyes. "You're such a beautiful daughter. I'm so proud of you, Cindy."

My mother had black, wavy hair. It brushed her shoulders when she moved her head. Her eyes were green and her complexion smooth and creamy looking. She was slender and wearing black slacks with a black tank top and a black- and white-striped blazer. Pearl earrings dangled from her ears and danced with the movement of her head. She was the most beautiful woman I had ever seen.

"You guys better get going or you're going to use up your half hour right here in the middle of the living room." Justine's sharp voice broke the spell.

We lived in Cornelius Pass, north of Hillsboro, Oregon, way out in the country. About 10 miles away was a ramshackle mom-and-pop grocery store, a gas station and a tiny diner. We decided to go into the diner. We took a seat at one of the old Formica dinette tables, and I sat as close as possible to my mother. We talked a little bit, but how much can you say in less than a half hour? My mom glanced at her watch every few minutes, and when she said it was time to go, I just couldn't believe it. That was it? This was all I was going to enjoy of my mother?

As we walked to the car, I held her hand.

THE UNCHAINED

"Mama, take me with you. I want to live with you."

Gathering me close, she started to cry. She tried to make me understand. "Cindy. Oh, I know how difficult it is for you to understand, my angel, but I can't do that. I don't earn enough money to take care of you. And if I took you with me, it wouldn't be fair not to take Bill and David, too. I love them just like I love you." She paused to give Bill a loving and reassuring look. "When your father and I divorced, he told me he would never let me split you kids up, and now I think he was right about that. The three of you are a family together."

We drove to my father's house in silence, all of us lost in our own thoughts. When we pulled up in front of the house, we got out of the car, my mother walked around the front of it and we all hugged and said our goodbyes.

"I promise I will come back and visit again. And next time, we'll arrange to share the whole day together."

She drove off, and I just stood there watching. Even after I could no longer see her car, I continued to watch. I believed if I stood there long enough, she would turn around and come back for me.

She didn't.

I was distracted by the honking of a horn and Justine yelling at me out the car window. "Cindy, are you going to stand there all night? Come get in the car. We're going to be late for Bill's meeting."

About three days after my mother's visit, we had just gone to bed and I could hear my father and stepmother arguing. After things settled down, my father got both Bill and me up and made us come out to the living room and sit on the couch. Justine was sitting in a big armchair with that smirk on her face. My father stood in the middle of the room.

"I want you both to call Justine Mom."

Bill didn't say a word, but I erupted.

"But she's not our mom! We just had a visit with our mom."

Justine couldn't contain herself. "Who cooks your food, does your laundry, carts you around wherever you have to go — wipes your snotty noses?"

She glanced at my father as if to say, "Well? Aren't you going to back me up?"

My father looked very uncomfortable, but he told us we had to do it.

"Cindy, let me hear you call her Mom. Now."

I was horrified, and I felt trapped. He was on her side. On the verge of panic and aware of a tremendous feeling of disloyalty, I barely got the word out. "Mom." That was it. Just that one word. Bill quickly followed suit. Although I had to call her that, I never felt that way about her.

Two weeks later, my stepmother came and picked us up after school, and as we pulled into the driveway of the house, she spoke to us in a cold, detached voice. "You and Bill come into the living room and sit down right after you put your things away."

Uh oh. I wonder what I did now.

Bill and I joined her in the living room. She was sitting in the middle of the couch, and he sat on one side of her, and I sat on the other.

"Your mother has been murdered."

Neither Bill nor I said a word. We didn't even move.

"Did you hear what I said? Your mother has been murdered!"

Bill continued to sit quietly. I was horrified and began to fall apart.

"No!"

"Cindy, it's true whether you want it to be or not. You have to accept it."

Sobbing, I ran out of the room. "Leave me alone! Don't speak to me!"

Alone in my room, I tried to process this. *How can this be possible? Things like this only happen in the movies.* I was 8 years old.

My father tried to soothe me when he got home from work, but I rejected all his efforts. He shook his head and ran his hand through his thick hair as he quietly left my room.

We attended the funeral. Sitting in the backseat of the car, I gazed out the window but really didn't see anything.

When we got to the church, people were arriving, many of them crying, and everyone was finding a seat inside. Our family had the first two pews in front. The church was filled with flowers, and the heady scent made me feel a little dizzy. When I looked up to the front of the church, I saw a rectangular-shaped box, rather large, and flowers were draped all over it. My paternal grandfather told me it was a casket and Mama was lying inside. The lid was open, but I couldn't see anything from where we were sitting.

The pastor was performing the funeral service, so I wasn't allowed to talk. My head drooped, and silent tears ran from my eyes. I watched them splash onto my dark blue dress where they left little wet dots on the fabric.

Before I knew it, people were starting to get up. They made a line and started filing by the open casket.

"I want my mom! I want my mom!" My screams seemed to come from deep within my soul, and I was inconsolable.

Grandpa took my hand. "Do you want to see your mama?"

Nodding my head yes, I walked up to the front of the church with him. When we reached the casket, I looked inside and saw my mother. She looked so very beautiful. She was wearing a red outfit that set off her dark hair to perfection, and she held a single red rose in her hands. She looked like she was asleep.

A horrible scream that didn't even sound human resonated throughout the church, and people gasped in reaction. I reached out and grabbed the side of the casket.

"Mama, don't leave me!" I shrieked. "You promised to visit me again!"

Grandpa was beside himself and couldn't get me to let go of the side of the casket. My father hurried to his side. The hideous screaming continued. I didn't even realize it came from me. My father pried my fingers from the casket, lifted me up and carried me out of the church.

THE UNCHAINED

We went to a memorial dinner where people spoke in hushed tones while they ate. I heard my father talking to my grandpa. "I told you not to let her view the body, Dad."

"I know, but the poor little thing …"

"Oh, never mind. There's nothing we can do about it now."

I couldn't even think of eating. I was in shock, and everything was surreal. What I really wanted to do was return to the church and talk to my mom. As I wandered aimlessly through the big room, I became aware of an aunt of mine having a discussion with someone else about the details of my mother's murder. They were standing in a doorway, and I quickly hid myself within earshot by crouching down beside a big chair.

"Well, I think you heard she was going through another divorce. And she had another little boy about a year old."

The other woman made a clucking sound as if she was sympathizing.

"Caroline lived in an apartment, and she had a roommate. Some gal who worked at the same place she did. Well, there was this guy, a weirdo actually, who was stalking Caroline. They say he lived in the same apartment complex. He would walk by her place and bang on the window, knock on the door and ask to borrow the silliest things. He also left notes in her mailbox."

"Must have been a bad part of town," the other woman contributed.

"Well, I don't know, but finally her roommate got scared, told Caroline she didn't feel safe there anymore and moved out. Apparently, the court wouldn't let Caroline move until the divorce was settled. Caroline had a boyfriend, and he kept a close watch on her. They were going to get married."

"Good grief. Another marriage?"

"Yes. Well, one morning, Caroline didn't show up for work, and she didn't call, either. Caroline was always very punctual, so her friend got concerned, called the boyfriend and told him about it. He called Caroline, but there was no answer, so he rushed over to the apartment. He found her dead in the bathroom. But here's a positive note: her roommate was a Christian and had talked Caroline into attending church with her. A wonderful thing happened to her. In no time at all, Caroline accepted Jesus as her Lord and Savior, confessed her sins and gave her heart to him. It's wonderful that the family has the peace and reassurance that Caroline is in heaven with him now."

Everything went black as I slumped into a pile on the floor.

***

I was lonely, I felt unloved and I was isolated because of how far out in the country we lived. My primary activities were listening to music or writing poetry in my room and walking in the woods. I was a very sad little girl, and I did a lot of crying. I had to be careful about the tears because my stepmother didn't have much tolerance for them.

Our family didn't have a religious background, so I was surprised when my father thought it would be a good idea for Bill and me to go to church. The church had a bus that would pick kids up and take them, so we went. As I became more aware of the Lord and started learning all about him, I wanted him to take control of my life. While I was still 8 years old, I asked Jesus to forgive my sins and come into my heart. I know for certain he did. After that, I spent a good part of my time talking to God and singing to him, and I tried to live my life the way I knew he wanted.

While I was growing up, I thought about my mother a lot. I never stopped missing her, and I often talked to God about it.

"Why didn't I have a mother to live with, God?"

God sent me a dream. In the dream, I walked into a large room, and there were a lot of women walking around in there. I recognized a few of them. I saw a couple of aunts, my stepmother and a few other ladies who had contributed some mothering in my life. None of them spoke to me, and no one paid any attention to me. There was just no connection between us at all.

A few weeks later, God gave me another dream. He led me into a beautiful meadow. It was a bright, sunny day, and I could see someone across the meadow, quite a distance away. It was impossible to see who it was. As we approached each other, I saw it was my mother. She had a big smile on her face, and we embraced. She spread a blanket in the grass, and we sat down and enjoyed a picnic. Then she looked at me and told me she had to go. "No. Don't leave me." We cried together, and then she smiled and disappeared.

I knew immediately what God was telling me: "The reason you didn't connect with any of the mother figures in your life, Cindy, is because your mother is in heaven with me waiting for you. You will see her again, and then you will be with her forever." This instilled in me an amazing new hope and peace.

I met Steven when I was 17 and in high school. We dated until I graduated, and then we became engaged. Soon after we got married, I wanted to have a child. It took us a while, but eventually, I got pregnant, and we had a son named Trenton. I am ashamed to say I slid away from God and discontinued my walk with Jesus. As soon as I did, things started going terribly wrong in our marriage.

Both Steven and I became social drinkers. He was into drugs and pornography, and I became a cocaine user. We both started having affairs. I was aware of God through all of this, and although I felt convicted in my heart because of my sins, I refused to stop.

One night, the heavy weight of the direction of my life bore upon my soul, and God spoke to my heart: "If you don't stop this, you're going to die." I was sure he meant I would die not only physically, but spiritually, as well. I also think he meant I would lose my husband and child.

I'm convinced it was the hand of God that sent my

new neighbor to knock on my front door and introduce herself. I invited her in to talk, and before I knew it, I had poured out my heart to her. She was going to a church where she was very happy, and she invited me to go with her. The very next Sunday, I attended with her, and while I was there, I was introduced to a woman who was a Christian counselor.

After a few sessions with the counselor, my heart and mind began to clear. The light of my life began to dawn once again, and I rededicated my life to Jesus. I gave everything to the Lord. I got my drug paraphernalia and my cigarettes and laid all of it out on the coffee table at home. Then I broke down and cried. "Lord, I give these to you. I don't want them in my life, and I know you don't want them in my life."

Wondrously, we experienced a great healing in our marriage. About a month after my rededication to Jesus, Steven gave his heart to the Lord. He gave up pornography and drugs, and we both decided to renew our marriage vows. We were starting over again — falling in love, once more, with each other and with Jesus.

About two years after giving birth to Trenton, I wanted to have another child. There was a problem. His birth had been very traumatic, and, in the end, I had to have a caesarean section. The whole experience upset me so much, I got my tubes cauterized to prevent future pregnancies.

A friend of mine at church told me her husband had a vasectomy reversal, and it worked for them. To my absolute delight, after looking into it, I learned it could be done, and I had surgery to reopen my tubes.

We tried without success to have another child, so I took fertility drugs for about two years. When that didn't work, I became despondent.

We decided to give in vitro fertilization a try. When we didn't get pregnant the first time, Steven just wanted to give up.

We were discussing it one night, and I blurted out, "We have to have a baby because I know we are supposed to have a daughter."

"You *know?* How do you know?"

"Because right before we were married, God sent me a dream, and it's been a recurring dream ever since."

He leaned forward on the ottoman, hands clasped between his knees. "Tell me about it."

"It starts as a very fuzzy picture, and I try hard to figure out what it is. Gradually, it becomes clear enough for me to see you, me and a little girl."

He agreed to try again.

One Wednesday night, I was at church, and we were trying to come up with a name for a choir group. A lady stood up and exclaimed with great excitement, "Shekinah! Shekinah Glory!"

"What's that?" I asked the music pastor.

"It means 'God's glory.'"

I knew instantly I was pregnant with our daughter, and God wanted us to name her Shekinah.

The next day, as I sat in the waiting room at the doctor's office, I was glancing through a magazine. My atten-

THE UNCHAINED

tion was drawn to an article titled "Glory." As I read it, I learned all about the miraculous development of a yellow African violet. The man who developed it was a student of plant genetics and a Christian. He said God told him to trust him regarding the yellow African violet. Although scientists had been reaching for that dream for 50 years and their research told them it would be impossible to produce, he believed what God said. It took a long time, but finally, the yellow African violet was born.

For a few minutes, I pondered the similarities between trusting God for the yellow African violet and my great desire to have a daughter. The previous evening, God had given me part of her name: Shekinah. I now knew her middle name: Glory. God told me I would have a daughter, and in spite of any odds, I believed him.

My gaze returned to the article. The author said, "God gave me some scripture as the basis for our faith. It was Matthew 19:26."

"Humanly speaking, it is impossible. But with God, everything is possible."

When I saw the doctor, he told me I was pregnant. I smiled. "I know. Her name is Shekinah Glory."

"Well, we don't know the sex of the child yet."

"Yes, 'we' do."

He scratched his head as I flashed him a big smile and walked out of the office. In my car, I took a moment to write something to my daughter across the top of the article. I wanted her to read it, and I wanted to tell her the whole story when she was old enough to understand.

"Shekinah, this story inspired me like nothing else ever did in truly believing God for you."

All the way home, I prayed with thanksgiving to Jesus. Through him there had been so much healing and so many blessings. "Lord, thank you for always keeping your promises of love to us. Thank you for the gift of this child. Steven and I promise to raise Shekinah and Trenton so they will know you, Lord." As it turned out, God, in his infinite wisdom, provided us the opportunity to fulfill our vow — I delivered a baby girl.

While I was pulling into our driveway, a bit of scripture ran through my head:

"Let the children come to me. Don't stop them! For the kingdom of heaven belongs to such as these." (Mathew 19:13-15)

CONCLUSION

If you, or someone you know, can relate to these stories, you are by no means alone. These are true accounts of Evergreen attendees who've experienced genuine life changes through a personal encounter with God and his life-changing love.

Do you struggle with thoughts like: *Can I experience such a life-changing encounter? Do I even deserve such freedom from my guilt, shame or the past? Is this kind of change and healing really possible for me?* It is our deep desire to help you discover the answer to these questions is, "Yes!" But the decision to believe and act on that is yours.

We want you to know that an encounter with God will lead to change in your life. It can and will happen whenever and wherever you are. The first step is to prayerfully ask Jesus to help you and be with you. There is no right or wrong way to pray. Just say some simple and honest words from your heart, such as:

Jesus, I am at a point where I know I cannot continue the way I am. I need change and willingly surrender myself and my life to you. I recognize that I have done wrong. Please forgive me of my wrongdoings and come into my heart. Now, lead my life and guide my daily decisions according to your will. Amen.

THE UNCHAINED

We invite you to join us at Evergreen Christian Center, where you will find that we are not so different and where we recognize the fact that life is often not fair. But we can live with great hope, peace and joy, even in the midst of our daily struggle. Our hope for you is that you, too, will experience the amazing gifts of God's grace: his dynamic, life-changing love, acceptance and forgiveness.

We would love for you to join us!
We meet Saturday evenings at 6 p.m. and
Sunday mornings at 9 and 11 a.m. at
4400 NW Glencoe Road, Hillsboro, OR 97124.

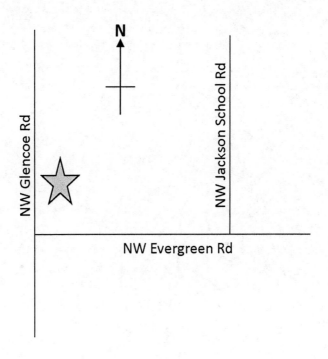

Please call us at 503.648.7168 for directions, or
contact us at www.eccfoursquare.org.

For more information on reaching your city with stories from your church, please contact Good Catch Publishing at www.goodcatchpublishing.com

GOOD CATCH PUBLISHING

Did one of these stories touch you?
Did one of these real people move you to tears?
Tell us (and them) about it on our reader blog at
www.goodcatchpublishing.blogspot.com.